MYSELF MUST I REMAKE

MYSELF

*The Life and Poetry
of W. B. Yeats*

MUST I REMAKE

by Gayatri Chakravorty Spivak

THOMAS Y. CROWELL COMPANY New York

11085

ACKNOWLEDGMENTS

The following poems are reprinted with permission of Macmillan Publishing Co., Inc. from *The Collected Poems of W. B. Yeats:* "A Woman Homer Sung," "No Second Troy," "The Fascination of What's Difficult," "On Those That Hated 'The Playboy of the Western World,'" "To A Wealthy Man Who Promised a Second Subscription to the Dublin Municipal Gallery If It Were Proved the People Wanted Pictures," "Paudeen," "The Magi," "A Coat," "Closing Rhymes," "On Being Asked for a War Poem," "A Deep-Sworn Vow," "The Second Coming," "To Be Carved on a Stone at Thoor Ballylee," "Meditations in Time of Civil War," "Two Songs from a Play," "The Tower," "Among School Children," "Blood and the Moon," "Coole Park and Ballylee," "At Algeciras—A Meditation Upon Death," "Gratitude to the Unknown Instructors," "Crazy Jane Talks with the Bishop," "There," "Meru," "Lapis Lazuli," "Sweet Dancer," "The Lover's Song," "Beautiful Lofty Things," "The Spur," "Long-Legged Fly," "The Statesman's Holiday," and "Under Ben Bulben." Copyright 1912, 1916, 1919, 1924, 1928, 1933, and 1934 by Macmillan Publishing Co., Inc. Copyright 1940 by Georgie Yeats. Copyright renewed 1940, 1944, 1947, 1952, 1961, 1962 by Bertha Georgia Yeats. Copyright renewed 1956 by Georgie Yeats. Copyright renewed 1968 by Bertha Georgie Yeats, Michael Butler Yeats, and Anne Yeats.

Designed by Mina Baylis Greenstein
Manufactured in the United States of America
Library of Congress Cataloging in Publication Data is on page 204.

ISBN 0-690-00114-2
1 2 3 4 5 6 7 8 9 10

Sivani Chakravorty
Her book

Contents

MYSELF MUST I REMAKE

CHAPTER I

Childhood and
Youth

I RELAND, that beautiful green island off the western coast of England, was ruled by the English for over eight hundred years. Although separated by a stretch of water never more than 130 miles wide, the two countries were vastly different. The people of Ireland were Gaels who belonged to the Celtic race, with a rich and distinctive mythological tradition. The people of England were predominantly Anglo-Norman or Anglo-Saxon, with a thoroughly different heritage. In the sixteenth century, England became Protestant. Ireland remained Catholic. England turned from being an agricultural country to a country of merchants, and finally industrialized herself. Ireland remained an agrarian, nearly wild land. Much of its thwarted development was due to England's harsh Irish policy.

At the end of the fifteenth century, for example, England's King Henry VII instituted the policy of sending his own personal deputy to govern Ireland, and thus undermined the independence of Ireland's Parliament.

In the seventeenth century, under Oliver Cromwell, the ruthless Puritan Protector of England, English fury was fully vented upon Ireland. Ireland was brought under strict military control. Much Irish land was confiscated. Irish noblemen and peasantry alike were driven into the woods. The already harsh laws against the Catholics were rigidly enforced. A Catholic could not own land or even a horse; he could not hold a commission in the army or choose to study for a profession like medicine or law. He could not teach. Often Catholicism was kept alive by priests on the run who would say Mass in the woods or on hillsides. The state of the Gaelic peasantry was of unmitigated wretchedness.

The Irish countryside was generally in the hands of English landowners who had acquired large holdings in Ireland. They leased out the land in tiny lots to native Irish farmers, who had no rights to the land they tilled, who often paid exorbitant rent for that land, and who could sometimes be evicted from it at the owner's will. The landowners were the Anglo-Irish, a predominantly Protestant "ruling class" who preserved an alien civilization upon Irish soil. At best, they were benevolent, paternalistic; at worst, cruel exploiters.

The benevolent ones were usually minor landowners

or the old Catholic aristocracy. They established a humane and amicable relationship with the Irish peasantry. William Butler Yeats was the descendant of minor landowning people—a family of merchants and soldiers, but mostly churchmen and scholars. They had come to County Sligo, Ireland, from Yorkshire, England, probably in the seventeenth century. They bequeathed to Yeats a real concern for the Irish, among whom he counted himself.

He was born on June 13, 1865, in a little row house in Sandymount, a suburb of Dublin. He was the eldest child of John Butler Yeats, at that time a brilliant and erratic law student, and Susan Pollexfen, a quiet and sweet woman with no interests outside her home.

Much of Yeats's childhood was spent in Sligo in the household of his maternal grandfather, "a silent and fierce old man," as the poet was later to write. After William was born, Susan Yeats had four other children—Elizabeth (Lolly), Susan (Lily), Robert, and John (Jack). The children's Pollexfen grandparents shared with Susan and John Butler Yeats the cares of bringing up a growing family. And so it was that Yeats came to think of Sligo as his home.

Sligo town is a tiny fishing port at the head of deep Sligo Bay on Ireland's gray Atlantic coast. The cobblestoned town lies between mountains—Ben Bulben, Knocknarea—and the sea. Yeats's father's grandfather, John Yeats, had been rector of nearby Drumcliff. Yeats himself was named after his father's father, also a clergyman, who had died three years before the poet's birth. His mother's father, William Pollexfen, was a small ship-owner, and later it was his ships that would bring the child back from England around the south coast of Ireland into Sligo. His childhood fancy was colored by sailors' stories and the turbulence of the North Atlantic.

Sligo is an area of lovely lakes—Lough Gill, in which is the little island of Innisfree; Lough Key; and many others. A few miles from his grandfather Pollexfen's house, "Merville," is Rosses Point, with its soft, grassy tongue of land projecting into the ocean. Against the pervasive fine Atlantic mist, the Sligo countryside has a jeweled, desolate, windy beauty.

It is as well an area of ancient ruins. Not only are there remains of castles, towers, churches, and massive crosses from the fourteen Christian centuries; there are also cairns and cromlechs (stone mounds and monuments) dating from Ireland's pre-Christian past. The most commanding is the huge cairn of the warrior-queen Maeve, which stands on top of Knocknarea, "the mountain of kings."

It is not surprising that Yeats was always to give his imaginative allegiance to this countryside. Here he encountered, in the formative time of childhood and adolescence, the roots of his own ancestral past as well as the roots of historic and mythic Ireland. The record of these years is found in *Reveries over Childhood and Youth* (1914), the opening book of his autobiography. Many of his poems, early and late, place themselves upon this landscape. The best-known Sligo poems are perhaps still the early ones like "The Stolen Child" or "The Lake Isle of Innisfree." In his middle and later years much of Yeats's poetry seems to move to exotic locales like Byzantium. But in fact, throughout his work, Yeats brings himself back to the Sligo countryside, "to that valley his fathers called their home."

His maternal grandfather was a very silent man who became for the young Yeats a symbol of authority. He was also a man of great personal courage. In *Reveries over Childhood and Youth* Yeats tells the story of how William Pollexfen single-handed saved the crew and passengers of a sinking ship in Sligo Bay one stormy night. A survivor later said of him, "I was not so much afraid of the sea as of that terrible man with his oar." His wife, Yeats's grandmother, was most gentle and helped the poor through many near anonymous acts of charity. She loved her garden and was young Willie's refuge. The house was full of many "grown-up uncles and aunts" who "came and went about their business" and many servants.

There also were a number of his father's relatives living in and around Sligo. Yeats recalls them in his autobiography. On the Yeats side was Mat Yeats, a great-uncle, and Mary Yeats, an unmarried great-aunt. They were proud of the military and clerical history of the Yeats family. The Pollexfens, his mother's people, had by contrast little use for family history. They were more concerned with money than were the Yeatses, and led careless, friendly, and active lives. On his mother's side there were also the Middletons, who owned flour mills jointly with the Pollexfens. "It was through the Middletons perhaps that I got my interest in country stories, and certainly the first faery stories that I heard were in the cottages about their houses." Among the Middletons he found the only companion of his own age, a little boy named George Middleton.

So thoroughly in the shadow of older people who loomed all around him, Yeats's childhood was lonely. The solitary imaginative child developed a habit of daydreaming and reverie.

In 1867 John Butler Yeats, who had passed his law examinations and been called to the bar, had decided to go to England and pursue art as a career.

In 1874, when William was nine, he had the chance to lodge with his father and a number of other painters at Burnham Beeches, a beautiful wooded area on the outskirts of London. There John Butler Yeats began painting the picture of a pond. Some of his eccentricity, his carefree attitude toward life, as well as his extreme commitment to his art, comes through in the well-known story of why the painting was never finished: "He began it in spring and painted all through the year, the picture changing with the seasons, and gave it up unfinished when he had painted the snow upon the heath-covered banks." Wanting to paint the pond as it really was, he had changed his picture with the seasons. And once he had explored it in all its aspects, he felt no need to complete the portrait.

John Butler Yeats was an extraordinary man. From his clergyman father he had inherited a habit of deep self-examination. By nature he was sociable, a persuasive talker. The persuasive, talkative, public profession of a lawyer had been chosen for him. But, after successfully studying for it, he chose for himself the solitary intro-spective career of a painter.

The decision reflected a certain change that had taken place in his mind. Born at a time when the most sensitive people were questioning the use of religion as merely a consolation against the hardships of life, he came to re-ject, as an undergraduate at Dublin's Trinity College, the institutions of Christianity. The contemporary Protestant church seemed to him to be a strange mixture of pas-sionate personal evangelism and cautious establishmen-tarianism whose members went through the motions of an outdated faith because of the attendant social advantages. Yet he could not reject the need for faith. He felt too emphatically that, in order to lead a meaningful life, a man must discover some grounds of belief. Examining his own conscience and the world around him, he gradually came to the conclusion that a man's self must be the repository of his faith. He must search out the nature of his self, and devote his energies to the fullest expres-sion of that self. For John Butler Yeats, it was the making of art that allowed this profound self-expression, and so it was that this excellent debater and student turned from law to art.

It follows that he was not interested in making money and that his son's youth was spent in relative poverty. Yet what he gave to his children was far more significant: the habit of using their creative imagination. Each Yeats child used this gift in his or her own way, according to his or her capacities. William became a great poet; Jack, an excellent painter; Lily and Lolly devoted themselves to creative crafts and inaugurated the Cuala Press, an art press that left its mark on Irish literary life.

When John Butler Yeats joined Heatherleigh's Art School in London in 1867, Pre-Raphaelitism was the most powerful antiestablishmentarian artistic movement. Pre-Raphaelite painters like Dante Gabriel Rossetti, Holman Hunt, and John Everett Millais were in rebellion against the extreme ugliness and standardization of industrialized England. They sought to restore to the art of painting a deep personal commitment on the part of the artist. They thought that in the work of the great sixteenth-century artist Raphael, painting had for the first time been divorced from the artist's beliefs, had become simply a special skill with undue emphasis placed on technique. Whether they were correct in this assessment or not, they looked to the Middle Ages—the period before Raphael, hence the name "Pre-Raphaelite"—as the great age of art when painting represented a way of life and belief. Their motto was Truth to Nature. In fact the hallmarks of Pre-Raphaelite painting were exact and precise rendering of the minutest detail and a vibrant luminosity of color.

These tenets went well with John Butler Yeats's enthusiasm for self-expression. He became a Pre-Raphaelite painter of promise. Indeed his work was so promising that Dante Gabriel Rossetti, one of the founders of the movement, sent for him. But John Yeats had an almost superstitious fear of becoming someone else's disciple; he did not answer Rossetti's summons.

As a father, he was fiercely loving and sometimes intellectually tyrannical. Some critics say his shadow fell across Yeats's entire poetic, intellectual, and personal life. He was very interested in the future poet's education. When Yeats was a small boy in Ireland, his father read aloud to him from *The Lays of Ancient Rome* by Lord Macaulay and *The Lay of the Last Minstrel* by Sir Walter Scott, and told him the plots of some of the volumes of *La comédie humaine* (*The Human Comedy*) by the great French novelist Honoré de Balzac. Preferring natural expression to all else, he forbade Yeats's first schoolmistress to teach the boy to sing in the artificially high nasal voice she favored.

At Burnham Beeches, and for about a year thereafter, Yeats's education was completely in his father's hands. To be a teacher of the very young requires a special patience which the strong-willed and demanding John Butler Yeats lacked. Conflicts inevitably resulted. Finally, after the family had been together in London for about a year, Yeats was enrolled at the Godolphin School, an exacting and unimaginative grammar school in Hammersmith. Here he felt for the first time English prejudice against the Irish, a nation then thought to be composed of wild hotheaded boors. Imagination came to the rescue: "I did not know what it was to be alone, for I could wander . . . imagining ships going in and out among the reeds and thinking of Sligo or of strange sea-faring adventures in the fine ship I should launch when I grew up."

These were the middle years of Queen Victoria's reign. All over England, established society lived in an atmosphere of heavy propriety. The extreme decorousness of social behavior was matched by the massive maroon and purple velvet curtains with ball fringes, the vast furniture of dark wood upholstered in similar fabric, the quantities of cast iron and polished brass, that decorated mid-Victorian interiors. The exteriors of houses were, more often than not, grotesquely carved, crenellated, and buttressed imitations of Gothic architecture. The tightly corseted women were encased in skirts of fantastic shape that hid all but the tips of their boots.

Artistic skills were being put to work against this artificial mode of morals, architecture, and dress. One of the examples of the success of such endeavors was to be found in London's Bedford Park, where the Yeats family took a house in 1876.

The houses in Bedford Park were designed by Sir Richard Norman Shaw, one of England's most brilliant architects. In Bedford Park, all was plain, cottagelike, picturesque, and as much as possible the handiwork of local craftsmen. The dominant colors were white, dull gold, peacock blue. The people who lived there were artists, or at least socially unconventional. The women dressed in long simple dresses that stressed the freedom of the body's movements, and the men went in for restrained flamboyance. To the influence of the fishing port of Sligo, the cloudy yet gentle West Irish countryside, and the remote authority of the chaotic household at Merville, was now added the influence of this rather strange phenomenon of Bedford Park.

At home the young Yeats was exposed to his father's constant presence and the presence of his father's friends, mostly painters who had at least started out as loyal Pre-Raphaelites. Upon Willie's youthful mind the ideals of Pre-Raphaelitism took a firm hold even before he was old enough to accept its doctrine.

The family returned to Ireland in 1880, "partly for financial reasons," and took a thatched house on the cliffs at Howth, just outside the city of Dublin. Yeats was sent to a school on Harcourt Street in Dublin that required of its students hard work and deep study. His record was eccentric. Once again his father attempted to interfere with the way the school was handling Willie's education, this time with little success. Willie's consuming interest was natural history. He prowled into caves and over cliffs in search of rare specimens. He kept a record of the habits of seabirds throughout the seasons, apparently because he planned to write a sea-going play; this finally became *The Shadowy Waters*.

Thwarted in influencing his son's academic curriculum, John Butler Yeats undertook a more far-reaching program. Now sixteen, the young Yeats had grown beyond the age when tact and patience form the greater part of teaching. Father could talk to son on his normal intellectual level, and son would accelerate to keep up with him. They often talked about the nature of the language of poetry. In a vivid paragraph in *Reveries over*

Childhood and Youth, Yeats recounts some early-morning conversations when his father discoursed on what constituted a good literary style. His standards were not concerned with external rules of writing. They were related, rather, to his central interest: the value of expressing the fullness of the individual personality. A style of writing that could capture the individual self in a heightened and impassioned state was therefore the one he most recommended to his son. He was not in favor of poetry that explained and presented abstract ideas. This led him to discredit most poetry of the Victorian period and much of the poetry of William Wordsworth, although he did admire that part of Wordsworth's poetry that seemed written out of genuine passion. Yeats was to carry these theories about the value of the expression of personality in art and literature, as well as many of his father's literary tastes, into later life. He was to remember how his father had proved his points about value in style with readings from poetry: the opening speeches of Percy Bysshe Shelley's poem *Prometheus Unbound,* scenes from Shakespeare.

Also at this time, the young Yeats became increasingly interested in the supernatural. He had grown up a lonely boy in a place where people believed in the existence of second sight, in benevolent and malevolent spirits who interfered with the lives of men and women in unpredictable ways. They believed, for example, that if a child was very beautiful, the fairies might steal him away to make him one of their own. They also believed in the existence of great ghostly kings and queens like Cuchulain (pronounced *Ku-hú-len*) and Maeve—folk versions of legendary heroes belonging to Celtic pre-Christian myth. These beliefs and the mysteriously beautiful Irish countryside left an indelible imprint upon his young wondering mind. There was thus a natural propensity in him to say, Yes, there is another hidden world beyond the visible world, and there is a meaning underlying the mechanisms of nature; it is a meaning we cannot usually fathom, but if we are attentive, we can spot clues to the secret workings of this world beyond our senses. He became curious about these clues. The curiosity was strengthened by his friendship with his uncle George Pollexfen, a serious student of astrology, a discipline that believes that the stars exert an inexorable influence upon human life. Youthful interest in such beliefs—that human affairs are under constant supernatural control—might at first seem trivial. Yet it is an early sign of Yeats's deepest questionings of the self and the world, questionings that were to lead to much of his most splendid poetic achievements. Certainly it persisted throughout his life.

But the most important event at this time in Yeats's interior life was his sudden sense of his own uniqueness. He sometimes felt, quite unreasonably, that all eyes were upon him. He began to be acutely aware of imagined awkwardnesses in himself. He began to be acutely concerned about his inner development too. And perhaps as a combined result of the awareness and the concern, he began to write poetry, more particularly poetic drama, seriously. This is how he puts it in *Reveries:* "I began to make blunders when I paid . . . visits, . . . and when I was alone I exaggerated my blunders and was miserable. I had begun to write poetry in imitation of Shelley and of Edmund Spenser, play after play—for my father exalted dramatic poetry above all other kinds. . . . I thought that having conquered bodily desire and the inclination of my mind towards women and love, I should live, as Thoreau lived, seeking wisdom."

In 1883, when he was eighteen, Yeats became a student at the Metropolitan School of Art in Dublin. His father came by to give an occasional lesson at the school. Most of the teachers held conventional academic views of art, in contrast to which J. B. Yeats's boldness stood out.

His father had expected him to go to Dublin's famous Trinity College, and Yeats later declared that he had not done so because it would have been too restrictive and conventional a step. He proposed to become a painter with poetry as his avocation—hence the art school. But the actual reason was that he had been unable to meet Trinity's entrance requirements in classics and mathematics. All his life Yeats was to have a peculiar awe of scholarship. Yet it is hard to say that a systematically imparted and acquired learning would not have spoiled the quality of a poetry greatly enriched by Yeats's later imaginative hoarding of philosophy, history, and systems of metaphysics.

With his attendance at art school a new stage in his

life began. From that period we can date his first independent friendships, associations, activities.

He found two close friends during this period of his
life: George Russell (who was to take the pen name
AE) and John O'Leary.

Russell, a fellow art student, had the gift of seeing in
waking life unreal scenes so vividly that they seemed
real. He was, in other words, a mystic and a visionary;
he drew and painted what he saw in his visions. The
regimen at art school did not suit him, and he left shortly
after Yeats came. But the two young men had already
formed a friendship, which was soon to find expression
in their joint dealings in Theosophy, a belief that God
can be known directly through visionary insight or
philosophical questioning.

In John O'Leary, a man in his fifties, Yeats found one
of the last representatives of what he later called "romantic Ireland," an Ireland whose people were dedicated, even to the point of sacrificing their very lives, to
their country's liberation from England. An upsurge of
such feeling had occurred in the middle of the nineteenth
century. Two reasons stand out among many as the cause
of this upsurge. In the 1820's the great Irish leader
Daniel O'Connell had aroused in the Catholic peasantry
a longing for freedom from British rule. And the potato
famine of 1845-50 had sent four million Irish poor, who
were almost totally dependent on the potato for food,
either to their graves or to the United States. The Irish
in America helped the Irish in their native land to or-

ganize against the English. The result was the Irish
revolutionary movement, the Fenian movement of the
1850's and 60's, a movement that collapsed in 1867 because of internal dissension provoked by the British.

In the 1870's and 80's, the spirit of the Fenian movement came alive again in the group known as the Irish
Republican Brotherhood. Like the Fenians, the Republican Brotherhood was uncompromising in its demand for
independence from England. Like them too, it drew much
of its support from Irishmen abroad, in America, for
example, and in Australia. Like the Fenians—who had
succeeded, through propaganda, in bringing the cause of
Ireland to public attention—the I.R.B. was chiefly interested in raising the consciousness of the Western world
to a full awareness of Ireland's justified longing for
freedom.

To complete the picture it should be mentioned that,
in addition to the Republicans, whose chief interest
was much-needed publicity about, rather than direct im-
provement of, the lot of the Irish, there was also, in the
1860's and 70's, a strong urban Catholic movement which
sought equal rights for the Irish within the British power
structure.

But not until the emergence of Charles Stewart Parnell—a leader able to unite the various warring factions
among the Irish themselves—could the country seem to
be able to look forward to real redress. Although this
Irish Protestant leader was a member of the British Parliament, he worked, often ruthlessly, for two ends: Irish

self-government and protection of the tenant peasantry from financial exploitation and eviction from the lands they farmed. Parnell, however, fell from power in 1890 because he loved Katherine O'Shea, a married woman. He was involved in the divorce case her husband brought against her, and thereafter married her. After the leader's fall and subsequent death, the revolutionary fervor seemed extinguished. Indeed it has been said that with the loss of political hope Irish patriots turned their energies to the arts and thus opened the way for a literary and artistic rebirth in Ireland.

John O'Leary's active participation in the Fenian movement had caused his imprisonment and then exile for fifteen years. Now head of the rejuvenated Fenian brotherhood, he shared a house with his sister, Ellen O'Leary, a minor poet. His personal standard of right and wrong was as lofty and austere, Yeats felt, as that of the noble Greeks and Romans about whose lives Plutarch had written. It was a mark of his fineness that he yielded to Yeats, who was barely in his twenties, in literary matters. At O'Leary's house Yeats met Douglas Hyde, an enthusiast of the Gaelic language, and future President of the Irish Free State; Katharine Tynan, a young poet with whom he would form a fairly long friendship; and John F. Taylor. Taylor was one of O'Leary's especial disciples, a man as rancorous and obstinate as O'Leary was gentle. According to Yeats, Taylor took an instant dislike to him. Yet Taylor occupied a significant place in Yeats's memory, for he was perhaps the most splendid

orator the poet was ever to hear. When the spell of impassioned eloquence was on Taylor, the gift of his rhe-
toric seemed to make him the inhabitant of a region far
removed from the pitiful imperfections of his daily personality. In Dublin, where oratory is a specially prized
art, Taylor had a strong reputation. Yeats's poetic ear
caught from Taylor the lesson of rhythm as an expression of passion. "His delivery . . . gave me a conviction
of how great might be the effect of verse, spoken by a
man almost rhythm-drunk, at some moment of intensity,
the apex of long mounting thought." This tribute is
especially meaningful because in some of his greatest
poetry Yeats came to possess that high poetic style which
seems made for passionate declamation.

But to speak of the full achievement of that high style
is to look forward forty years. The poetry Yeats was
writing during the 1880's was the halting, derivative,
self-conscious, yet promising work of the gifted novice
trying to find his own voice. As we have already seen,
his chief idols were the sixteenth-century poet Edmund
Spenser and the nineteenth-century poet Percy Bysshe
Shelley. Under his father's influence, much of the poetry
he wrote was dramatic verse.

Chief among his self-styled Spenserian efforts was the
poetic drama *The Island of Statues* (1885). Yeats does
not really capture the spirit of Spenser in this play. The
obvious borrowings are the pastoral Arcadian setting,
the pervasive archaism in language, and the peppering
of classical allusions. The following lines will serve as
well as any others to display the resulting stiffness:

Come forth: the morn is fair; as from the pyre
Of sad Queen Dido shone the lapping fire
Unto the wanderer's ships, or as day fills
The brazen sky, so blaze the daffodills;
As Argive Clytemnestra saw out-burn
The flagrant signal of her lord's return,
Afar, clear-shining on the herald hills,
In vale and dell so blaze the daffodills;
As when upon her cloud-o'er-muffled steep
Oenone saw the fires of Troia leap,
And laugh'd, so, so along the bubbling rills
In lemon-tinted lines, so blaze the daffodills.

It is difficult to believe that these lines are spoken by a shepherd, and that they describe nothing more than a field of daffodils!

Yet it is not enough to snicker at *The Island of Statues*. The overworked texture of the poem does show a real love for the flow of language and for the possibility of poetic beauty. The play's theme—how a poet rescues the victim of a vile enchantress and wins the hand of the good fairy—indicates allegorically Yeats's deep faith in the poet's calling. The proofs of this faith make the play stand out among the mass of Yeats's youthful writings.

Among Yeats's early Shelleyan efforts should be counted political poems like "The Two Titans" (1886) and the semipolitical verse play *Mosada* (1886). In *Prometheus Unbound*, Shelley had used the ancient Greek myth of Prometheus to express his own revolutionary political ideas. In "The Two Titans," Yeats presents two figures who superficially resemble Prometheus. But Yeats cannot yet sustain a political theme. He achieves nothing more than a general air of revolutionary sentiment.

Among the earlier nineteenth-century poets, Shelley was nearly unique in his use of blank verse—the favorite dramatic form of the Elizabethans—to express tragic and obsessive character conflicts. In his turn, Yeats imitates Shelley's imitation of a somewhat archaic convention.

Although as a play *Mosada* is lightweight—a saintly Moorish girl is burned at the stake for witchcraft by her former lover, now turned monk—it does contain some of Yeats's best work in these very early years. Yeats uses competently the Pre-Raphaelite formula for medievalistic, langorous, quaintly simple scene painting in verse:

> There in a dell,
> A lily-blanchèd place, she sat and sang,
> And in her singing wove around her head
> White lilies, and her song flew forth afar
> Along the sea.

His father was most enthusiastic about Yeats's work. He had *Mosada* privately printed and distributed. Among its readers were such eminent people as the poet Gerard Manley Hopkins and the critic Edward Dowden (neither of whom liked it).

Little by little Yeats began to try himself out as a speaker. He was a shy young man and put the public self-possession he lacked above all virtues. He spoke sometimes at informal discussions held by the Contemporary Club, founded by Charles H. Oldham of Trinity College, where the talk was about socialism or philosophy. But more significant than this were his ventures into oratory, and leadership at the Dublin Hermetic Society and the Young Ireland Society.

With George Russell and Charles Johnston, a school friend, Yeats founded in 1885 the Dublin Hermetic Society. (The name celebrated Hermes Trismegistus, the mythic Egyptian god-magician-philosopher.) The goal was to study the occult—magical, mystic, spiritualist thought—and Eastern philosophy in the belief that such study could reveal the existence of a life beyond the one that we can test through reason and the senses. The group examined legends of the supernatural and accounts of miracles for hints of this extrasensory life. One of the books these young people were most impressed by was A. P. Sinnett's *Esoteric Buddhism*, which seemed to provide a way out of the materialism and rationalism of mid-Victorian Britain, an age they thought rich in wealth but poor in spirit. In Yeats's personal case, perhaps his interest in such matters was also a reaction against an intellectually dominating yet ever kind father who saw no possibility of faith except in art and self-expression.

If the Dublin Hermetic Society represented Yeats's interest in occult studies, the Young Ireland Society reflected his other consuming interest, and indeed the consuming interest of many Irishmen at the turn of the century—the shaping of a unified national identity for

Ireland. The society had been formed on the model of the Young Ireland Society of the mid-nineteenth century. Its goal was to encourage young men and women to develop within themselves that dedication toward their country without which there was no hope of freedom from colonial rule. At their meetings Yeats tried to convince his rather commonsensical associates that good literature was indeed as important to the movement as political action, and that fine poetry can restore to the soul of a nation its own bright image.

In 1887, then, when he moved to London once again with his family, Yeats was already, at twenty-two, a working poet with an active life of the mind. Born in a country that was struggling to free itself and become a nation, he gave his youthful sympathies to help that country form a self-image worthy of respect. Born at a time when the young sensitive nonconformist found himself in serious reaction against the extravagant rationality of the British Establishment in the mid-nineteenth century, he had already struck out for a magical faith, unlike his father's skepticism, and unlike the highly institutionalized Christianity of his Protestant forebears. In appearance he was an incipient dandy—wearing his father's discarded many-tiered cape, long flared trousers that dragged at the heels, a flowing Byronic tie.

He was ready, in fact, to take the plunge into London's literary life.

CHAPTER 2

Imagination in the
Making

ONDON! The literary atmosphere of the city inspired the young man's awe. Yeats had just begun to feel his way about in Dublin, and now here was a new fortress to be taken! Impressing the extremely competitive London literary world with his creative worth was not, however, his only concern. There was also the problem of earning his own livelihood, for, as we have already learned, John Butler Yeats, his father, was not a financial success.

Yeats worked hard at odd jobs. He copied a fifteenth-century manuscript of *Aesop's Fables* for an English publisher. (In those days, before methods of duplication had been developed, this was the only way to get a rare manuscript ready for reprinting.) He wrote reviews for lesser- and gradually better-known journals. In 1888, he managed to get commissions from Irish and British publishers to compile books of Irish folk tales, ballads, and poetry. His fees were not large. The situation improved somewhat when in 1889 John O'Leary arranged for him to become the Irish correspondent for the *Boston Pilot* and the *Providence Sunday Journal*, papers which had already published his poems. He wrote pieces that dealt with Irish legendary and literary figures. As an Irishman describing his heritage to a sympathetic American audience, the twenty-four-year-old Yeats found a unique opportunity to fashion an image of Ireland, a country rich in ancient traditions.

Meanwhile, in 1887, his work was published for the first time in an English journal, *The Leisure Hour*. The poem was "King Goll," a wild and melancholy ballad. But his most important labor during the period from 1886 to 1888 was over a long poem.

Long narrative poems were then common undertakings. What is significant and uncommon is that Yeats did not choose a legend of King Arthur as Tennyson and Swinburne had, nor a Greek or Persian myth as Matthew Arnold had, nor an imaginary Arcadian pastoral as he himself had written earlier under Edmund Spenser's influence. His theme was Celtic. He wanted to make the riches of Ireland's legendary past accessible to the Irish reader and to the world. He also wanted to explore the significance of ancient Celtic symbols, objects like the spear, the tower, the hound with one red ear, that the pre-Christian Irish had endowed with mysterious mean-

ing. The finished poem came to some nine hundred lines
and left him totally exhausted. It was published in
Yeats's first book of verse, *The Wanderings of Oisin*
(pronounced *Usbéen*) *and Other Poems,* in 1889.

When we read the poem today, it seems a very old-
fashioned work, a legendary tale of no relevance to the
modern world. But as students of Yeats we find interest
in it, because it tells us so much about its maker and
represents so much progress in his way of writing.

Yeats found the legend in English versions of an
eighteenth-century poem written in Gaelic, the ancient
language of the Irish. Dialogues between Oisin and Saint
Patrick are not uncommon in older Irish literature. Oisin,
the son of Finn, the great Irish king, is lured away from
the world by Niamh (pronounced *Neebb*), a fairy prin-
cess, who takes him to the Island of Dancing, a place
of everlasting youth. Oisin remains enchanted by its
beauty and joy until, a hundred years later, a "staff of
wood from some dead warrior's broken lance" floating
on the tide brings back human memories, and the spell
is broken. Niamh then journeys with him to a second
island, called the Island of Victories. Here Oisin spends
another hundred years, fighting a frightful demon. When
the century is over, the sight of a floating beech branch
once again brings back memories of his human past.

> And then lost Niamh murmured, "Love, we go
> To the Island of Forgetfulness, for lo!
> The Islands of Dancing and of Victories
> Are empty of all power."

On the Island of Forgetfulness Oisin sleeps for a hundred years in the company of other immortals. But, at the end of the time, his dreams bring back remembrances of his life on earth three hundred years before. It is time for him to leave. Niamh has no other islands to offer him. He goes back to Ireland, with a promise to Niamh to return. She sets only one condition: his feet must not touch ground; if they do, he will become mortal and will not be able to return to fairyland.

The earthmen of three hundred years later seem very puny to Oisin, who is used to the grandeur of mythic heroes. He decides to return to Niamh. On his way back to her, he sees two men fall under a heavy sack of sand. He bends down, lifts up the sack, and flings it a great distance. His saddle girth breaks. He topples over. The horse runs off. The spell broken, he gets to his feet, a stooping, three-hundred-year-old man. To ask for the whereabouts of his family, his friends, his gods, he seeks out the wisest living man, Saint Patrick—for in the meantime Ireland has been Christianized. Patrick tells him that his heathen friends, family, and gods are suffering the tortures of eternal damnation. The poem ends with Oisin defiantly telling Saint Patrick that rather than go to Heaven he would prefer to join his own clan at death, "be they in flames or at feast."

Why was Yeats fascinated by this particular Celtic legend? Perhaps because it expressed, in part, many of his deepest questionings. One of these questions was, What is the relationship between the virtues praised in the legends of the pre-Christian culture of Ireland and the virtues praised in the doctrines of Christianity? The pre-Christian folktales and Celtic legends hold up the ideals of valor, physical heroism, physical beauty, and physical love. The asceticism of Ireland's Catholic saints and the institutionalized Protestantism of Victorian Britain seemed to hold up quite opposite ideals: meekness, self-sacrifice, spiritual beauty, and spiritual love. Oisin was the son of pre-Christian kings; Patrick, the father of Christian Ireland. In their confrontation Yeats saw embodied the contrast of two opposing sets of values. And in this poem at least, pagan heroism is given the last word.

Another thought that obsessed Yeats was: Does the decision to write poetry involve the supernatural? Is the poet something of a magician? Where do the poet's thoughts come from? From where does he receive the gift of creating an imaginary world out of mere words? Oisin is human, yet in love with a supernatural being. Does this reflect Yeats's suspicion that the all-too-human poet has connections with a world beyond this one? And the young poet also hints at some of his own self-doubtings. In the poem the world of the imagination is not self-sufficient. It is the memory of human reality that breaks Oisin's enchantment each time, prompting Niamh to lead him on to further islands of magic. Nor can the world of the imagination lead to real happiness. It can lead to pleasure (as on the first island), to successes and triumphs, even to a forgetting of one's sorrows. But, as Oisin asks Niamh:

> "And which of these
> Is the Island of Content?"

> "None know," she said;
> And on my bosom laid her weeping head.

"The Wanderings of Oisin," then, is the expression of complex themes through a symbolic story. In the manner of its telling, Yeats shows the beginnings of a real mastery of language. Many youthful influences are still in evidence, but, as the quotations show, he handles them with more assurance. In each of the three books of the poem, the style of writing changes markedly to duplicate the theme. In the first book, to match the languor of the beautiful bejeweled folk of the Island of Dancing, Yeats's verse has an overrhythmic, monotonous, songlike quality:

> On in the woods, away with them,
> Where white dewdrops in millions fall;
> On in the woods, away with them,
> Where tangling creepers every hour
> Blossom in some new crimson flower;
> On in the woods, away with them,
> Where trees made sudden cavern-glooms
> By roots that joined above our plumes—
> On in the woods, away with them!

In the second book, to match the subject of victorious combat, the poet successfully increases the rhythmic monotone until it is vaguely oppressive. The songlike quality is gone.

> Beyond the door a plain,
> Dusky and herbless, where a bubbling strain
> Rose from a little runnel on whose edge
> A dusky demon, dry as a withered sedge
> Swayed, crooning to himself in an unknown tongue.

But it is in the third book that Yeats's new-found poetic ingenuity is best seen. To match the perfect repose of the Island of Forgetfulness Yeats uses a long, undulating, anapestic rhythm made particularly famous by Algernon Charles Swinburne. Here is Yeats:

> In the roots of the grasses, the sorrels,
>   I laid my body as low;
> Sad Niamh came near me, and laid her brow on
>   the midst of my breast;
> And the horse was gone in the distance,
>   and years after years 'gan their flow;
> Square leaves of the ivy moved over us,
>   binding us down to our rest.

What is most interesting is that in this section Yeats is able to use the meter to convey not only the languor of sleep but also the weariness of old age. Oisin laments to Saint Patrick:

> Ah me! to be old without succour,
>   a show unto children, a stain;
> Without laughter, a coughing, alone
>   with remembrance and fear;
> All emptied of purple hours
>   as a beggar's cloak in the rain,
> As a grass seed crushed by a pebble,
>   as a wolf sucked under a weir.

In this long narrative poem, upon which he had worked so hard, Yeats began to show signs of real promise. "The Wanderings of Oisin" is his first significant work.

The "other poems" published in the volume containing "Oisin" were shorter. Although they seem to display many of the qualities of the earlier work we have discussed—Spenserian imitation, Shelleyan influences, attempts at picturesque simplicity—they also show signs of the poet's increasing skill. Poems such as "The Stolen Child" and "Down by the Salley Gardens" are good in their own right.

Meanwhile Yeats was becoming absorbed in some of the literary groups in end-of-the-century London. He was learning to speak their peculiar language, at the same time preserving and developing his distinct individuality.

His first move towards this literary world was a small one. In 1890, he urged John Todhunter, a friend of his father's, to write a play for the little local playhouse in Bedford Park, where the Yeats family had once again rented a house. At the rehearsals of the finally unspectacular performance, he met Florence Farr, a talented and beautiful amateur actress, whose lovely voice brought out in Yeats one of his lifelong convictions: poetry should be spoken musically; it should not sound like bastardized prose. The lady and the poet were later to make experiments in the proper recitation of verse, aided by the medieval musical instrument called the psaltery. His work with her affected not only his lyric poetry but his dramatic verse.

Also in 1890 he published "A Cradle Song" in the well-known *Scots Observer* magazine, and gradually he was drawn into the circle of writers, none of them yet famous, who gathered around William Ernest Henley, its editor. Henley was a man of strong tastes and temper, and by his pronouncements he influenced some of Yeats's literary opinions, as he did those of many of his "young men." Yeats published a good bit of his early verse in the *Scots Observer* and its successor, the *National Observer*.

At about this time, Yeats met and admired William Morris, the artist, designer, and writer. In Morris, who was now almost sixty, the Pre-Raphaelite interest in things medieval had found a full late flowering. In Morris's distinctive opinion the Middle Ages in Europe extended from the sixth to the fifteenth centuries. And he attributed the achievements of those thousand years to the growth and support of a perfectly integrated culture. The real secret of culture lay for Morris in the freedom of the artist and the craftsman. It was not through selfish individualism that this freedom was achieved. Medieval artists and craftsmen had banded together and formed cooperative societies which had ensured this freedom. The medieval artist was not interested in enhancing his own private reputation, nor was he the member of a minority. His strength was communal and collective. Morris also felt that, for medieval man, Church and State were united as two aspects of God's kingdom on earth. Because of this, art, religion, politics, and common life were united in an integrated world view. Morris contrasted this to modern society, where all is governed by commerce and the profit motive, and where specialization has increased so much that each man is solely interested in doing his own particular job and has no sense of society as a whole. In such a society the artist, suffering from a superiority complex, retreats to an ivory tower.

Morris tried actively to destroy artistic snobbery as well as the lack of public taste by bringing arts, crafts, and politics together. He designed furniture, tapestry, kitchen utensils, bookbindings, and many other objects, because he felt that beauty should be present in every aspect of living. His politics was Utopian, a sort of visionary socialism in which all men would be equal, deriving from society not reward for their labors but satisfaction of their needs. Yeats found himself attending meetings of the group of socialists and Utopians who gathered under Morris's leadership. Morris soon became Yeats's "chief of men." In him Yeats met one of the first examples of the all-around man. This ideal of a unified personality and a unified culture remained supremely important to Yeats throughout his life, and found expression in such important works as *A Vision* and the Byzantium poems.

In Morris and his Utopian socialism, Yeats found confirmation of his own belief, earlier strengthened by John O'Leary, that not only an individual but a whole people can achieve a unified identity, and that such an identity can be forged by the efforts of politically and culturally conscious men. His belief was, of course, not merely abstract. Ireland, denied fulfillment by centuries of political oppression and occupation by alien British social, political, cultural, and intellectual ideals imposed from without, seemed to be in need of such an identity, a "Unity of Culture" as Yeats put it. But he soon discovered a crucial difference between his own beliefs and those of Morris's group, named the Socialist League. The latter held that the identity of nations could be made over through a planned and active economic, artistic, social revolution. Religion, an inherited creed that tended to draw men back in time toward the past, seemed to these people an obstacle to such planning. Yeats, on the other hand, felt that changes in a people's identity must take place slowly and unself-consciously. If religion were imaginatively understood, not as a static code, but as a vision of the world that allowed men to think of a reality beyond that of the senses, it could help to unify a nation on the profoundest level, and give an anchor to planned changes. At the league's meetings, Yeats could not help blurting out his outrage a number of times at their outright rejection of religion. He drifted away from his association with them. He was still a very young man and was a little disappointed that Morris, who admired *The Wanderings of Oisin,* and who had understood and sympathized with his point of view, did not do more to encourage his followers to appreciate the power of spiritual things.

But Yeats was not only interested in making his mark in the London literary world. He also wanted to act independently as an Irish man of letters. His most ambitious undertaking in this respect was the founding of the Irish Literary Society of London in 1891 and the National Literary Society in Dublin in 1892.

He founded the two Irish societies impelled by the strength of his conviction that a country's national identity could be shaped by men of imagination. In this he was supported by the strong interest in Ireland's ancient mythology and literature that existed among Irish intellectuals and his own leanings toward Theosophy and the occult.

The men associated with the Irish and Irish-American revolutionary movements in the nineteenth century had been simple patriots, not artists or men of letters. Their taste in art and literature had given rise to a shallow, sentimental, pamphleteering kind of writing that had become the hallmark of Irish patriotism. Yeats wanted this situation changed. He wanted to inaugurate a way of writing that would combine the qualities of serious contemporary European literary forms with symbols from the mythology of pre-Christian Ireland or with the simple beauty of the legends and folktales of rural Ireland. Such a literature, he hoped, would lead every Irishman to find roots in his own land that were as noble as those Europe had found in Greece or Judea. Gaining support for his efforts was not an easy matter. Yeats was young, fiery, and often tactless. John O'Leary sometimes rebuked him, always guided him. To create a taste for good literature among the Irish, Yeats traveled to little Irish towns, trying to build up small impromptu libraries, and he negotiated with the publisher Fisher Unwin for a series of small books devoted to Irish matters.

The projected series ran into trouble at the very start. Sir Charles Gavan Duffy, Australian statesman and Irish patriot, a man in his seventies, had recently returned to his native Ireland after a long career in Australia, wishing to devote himself once more to the Irish cause. Although he was an able man, and had worked in his youth with the noted Irish leader Daniel O'Connell, he lacked literary taste. He maneuvered himself into a position of control over the contents of the series, and Yeats began to see an end to all his hopes. Now for the first time Yeats was to experience how unreasonably political victories may be won. Sir Charles had enemies in Ireland who had as little taste in literature as he. Yet these people supported Yeats's noble plans for the projected series, undermining Sir Charles's power. Nonetheless, the ill-fated series languished after the first few numbers. Yeats was unable to prevent the publication of a particularly dry piece of writing, which effectively killed public interest.

Among the few good things brought out in the series

was Douglas Hyde's *The Story of Early Gaelic Literature* and Standish O'Grady's *The Bog of Stars*. O'Grady, though a capable historian and one of the inspirers of the "Irish Renaissance," was yet a somewhat pathetic figure, for he at once supported and bitterly criticized the cause of the Anglo-Irish landed aristocracy—a group generally detested by the predominantly native and Catholic revolutionary movement—in a way that drew Yeats's lasting sympathy. Douglas Hyde was learned in Gaelic which, in its modern form, was then spoken by only a small percentage of the Irish peasantry. He founded the Gaelic League in 1893 which both with its publications and in its efforts to foster a knowledge of Gaelic in Ireland gained considerable popularity. Yeats saw in him the presence of the genuinely folk imagination. In later life, using the pen name of Craoibhin Aoibhin (pronounced *Créeb-hen Eéb-hen*, "the little branch") Hyde wrote poetry in Gaelic that delighted many nationalistic young people.

In 1894, at the little playhouse in Bedford Park, Yeats met Bernard Shaw, the gifted young Irish socialist and playwright. Yeats's own play, *The Land of Heart's Desire*, was put on the same bill with Shaw's celebrated *Arms and the Man*. Shaw's play was witty, commonsensical, and full of social criticism. Yeats's play was dreamlike and written in verse. Yeats dramatized in his play the contrast between, on the one hand, the pagan virtues of joy and the fulfillment of desire and, on the other, the Christian virtues of spiritual wisdom, as well as the social "virtues" of craftiness and selfishness. His main character was a fairy child who lures away the soul of a newly married bride. The setting is the aggressively simple, timeless interior of an Irish peasant cottage. To the late nineteenth-century British audience, Shaw's play seemed far more effective. Yeats had a fair way to go before acquiring a dramatic style that would retain its dreamlike characteristics and would, at the same time, grip an audience. In fact, Yeats would never quite understand Shaw's sort of writing, and he once had a dream in which Shaw appeared as a constantly smiling sewing machine. The dream, no doubt, reflected Yeats's view of Shaw as a mechanical and efficient playwright who gained his effects through unceasing wit and humor.

In 1890 Yeats played a leading part in the establishment of the Rhymers' Club. He was now living in rooms in Fountain Court in London. Across the hall, sharing a common entrance, lived Arthur Symons, poet, essayist, short-story writer, and translator and enthusiast of French literature. Symons became a close friend and associate, introducing Yeats to the casual urbanity of London life as well as to the ultramodern, half-mystical poetry of the French Symbolists. (In 1899, Symons dedicated his book *The Symbolist Movement in Literature* to Yeats.) Yeats felt himself ready for an exchange of ideas with his fellow poets in London, yet those whom he met seemed strangely shy and silent, rather indisposed to talk about poetry. Perhaps the founding of a club would loosen their tongues, Yeats thought. This was the origin of the Rhymers' Club, begun jointly by Yeats and Ernest Rhys, poet, critic, and editor. The group—

composed of Yeats, Rhys, Lionel Johnson, Ernest Dowson, Arthur Symons, and others—met in the upper room of a pub in Fleet Street called the Old Cheshire Cheese. The club never really developed into a forum for discussion, but the members did read much of their new works aloud. In *Reveries* Yeats has described the electric effect of hearing Lionel Johnson read his poem "By the Statue of King Charles at Charing Cross." The Rhymers' poetry can be seen in two volumes of *The Book of the Rhymers' Club.* In "The Grey Rock," a poem written long after the club had disbanded, Yeats commemorates his friendship with the Rhymers, addressing them as "Poets with whom I learned my trade, / Companions of the Cheshire Cheese. . . ."

Of all the members of the club, Lionel Johnson touched Yeats most closely. He was a pathetic, learned, dwarfish young man who led an extremely disciplined intellectual life and yet was a raging alcoholic. Early in their friendship Yeats discovered that this grave and gifted poet was also a pathological liar. And soon Johnson was dead of drink and melancholia.

In fact many of the members of the Rhymers' Club, many young London poets, were psychologically disturbed and died tragically. In the section of his autobiography entitled "The Tragic Generation," Yeats speculated about the reasons for this.

Perhaps, Yeats writes, it was because they were all followers of a philosophy of life represented by the doctrines of Walter Pater, one of the most important critics of the day. In the influential "Conclusion" to his book *Studies in the History of the Renaissance*, Pater wrote: "Not the fruit of experience, but experience itself, is the end. A counted number of pulses only is given to us of a variegated, dramatic life. How may we see in them all that is to be seen in them by the finest sense? How shall we pass most swiftly from point to point, and be present always at the focus where the greatest number of vital forces unite in their purest energy? To burn always with this, hard, gemlike flame, to maintain this ecstasy, is success in life."

An entire generation of young men took this as their motto. They tried to achieve "success in life" by living every waking moment in deliberate ecstasy. Often this led to a passion for elaborate detail but little sense of the over-all goals of one's way of life. Often too, because of the psychological effort required to live always at a very high pitch, these young men needed to escape into periods of dissipation. If, Yeats felt, such personalities could have found interest in some real issue outside themselves, the tendency toward self-destructive dissipation would have been arrested. In his own case, Yeats believed, participation in the cause of Irish independence, and an active involvement in occult practices, served as checks.

A solitary childhood, Pre-Raphaelitism, the occult, Irish politics—to this list of the elements that went to compose Yeats's early imagination, we add, then, a fifth: an immersion in the chronic melancholy of the turn of the century.

Aubrey Beardsley was another remarkable figure who

belonged to this group. Beardsley was an artist and illustrator who died of tuberculosis while still in his twenties. The importance of his influence upon today's
graphic art is unquestionable. At the time he was hounded
for his so-called obscenity, and the dynamic experimental
magazine *The Yellow Book* was closed down because his
bizarre illustrations to Oscar Wilde's *Salome* were published in it. His name was anathema in conservative
circles. Quite defiantly Yeats voiced strong public approval when Arthur Symons, on being asked to edit a
magazine called *The Savoy*, gave the publisher only one
condition: that Beardsley be its illustrator. The handsome magazine ran for eight issues, and published the
work of many illustrious writers.

All through this period of political and literary activity in the late 1880's and 90's, Yeats kept up his interest in the occult. He participated in séances, regularly
practiced trance meditation, read books on mysticism.
Some questions particularly occupied him: What exactly
was the nature of the images that haunted him in his
dreams, in his experiences with trance and mediumship,
in the making of poetry? What were the foundations of
the fairy and ghost lore of the country people he
encountered?

In 1888, after some second thoughts, he had become a
member of the Theosophical Society. Founded in 1875,
the Theosophical Society was an international group devoted to interpreting the texts of the world's religions
as accounts of truth about the life of the spirit and a
world beyond that of the senses. Morris had helped Yeats

understand the concept of Unity of Culture socio-
logically. The Theosophists helped him construct a spiritual explanation for this same concept.

The Theosophists believed that all religions shared
certain fundamental beliefs, that there were basic points
of similarity in their explanations of the world, which if
properly understood, would lead to a direct knowledge
of the Universal Oversoul. This common core, they
held, could be apprehended in what they called "the
Secret Doctrine," and to learn more about it, they devoted themselves to studying the mystical lore of various
esoteric religions. Mastery of the Secret Doctrine, pieced
together by their research, would form the basis for far
greater spiritual powers than man had ever known.

With his fascination with the supernatural and his
longing for Unity of Culture, Yeats found these beliefs
highly congenial. So far, so good. Just before he joined
the group, however, the Theosophical Society had suffered some discredit from the British Society for Psy-
chical Research. This was because the organization's
founder and leader, Helena Blavatsky, an elderly, buoy-
ant, mischievous woman, claimed to possess great psychic
powers. She could receive the Secret Doctrine directly,
she said, without need of research. When after some
hesitation Yeats joined the Theosophists, he found her
strong personality very engaging. He developed in his
own way, in his poetry and prose, what he learned from
the Theosophists about the basic unity of all religions.

In 1894, however, Yeats was compelled by the officers
of the society to leave because he wanted every credo

professed by the Theosophists to be scientifically docu-
mented. This eagerness to put things to the proof was one
of Yeats's outstanding characteristics and often earned
him the charge of naïveté.

A few months before leaving the society, Yeats met
Liddell Mathers, translator of occult texts and devotee
of occultism. Mathers was interested in the Cabala, the
so-called "doctrine received by word-of-mouth," a way
of interpreting the Bible that has been passed down
orally, supposedly since ancient times. All through Europe and the Middle East, rabbis and scholars had kept
the secret codes of this doctrine alive. The true and
hidden meanings of the Jewish and Christian Scriptures,
they believed, could be understood by those who knew
the codes. Some of the codes had been transmitted by
visual symbols or symbolic designs, which Yeats was to
find particularly interesting. Actively interested in the
supernatural since early youth, Yeats had of course
known of the Cabala, and through his association with
Mathers, he now became actively involved in cabalistic
studies.

Mathers had a hypnotic but unbalanced personality.
He half imagined for himself an illustrious Scots ancestry, and accordingly changed his name to MacGregor
Mathers, and finally to just MacGregor. He founded a
secret society called the Hermetic Order of the Golden
Dawn, the members of which were reputable men with
a deep interest in ancient cults of supernatural wisdom.
Rather than reject the heritage of the prescientific ages,
they wished to find out if there was any truth in these
occult teachings. They made the society a secret one to

protect themselves from public scoffing. Being an active member meant moving up through different stages of spiritual control, each stage marked by its own elaborate ritual initiation and names such as "Zelator" (enthusiast), "Adeptus" (adept), "Magus" (wise). Yeats, who joined the society in 1890 and reached the highest rank in 1915, was certainly most interested in the evocative power of cabalistic symbols. In 1894–95 he spent a long winter at the house of his astrologer uncle George Pollexfen in Sligo, and the two made certain experiments. Yeats's goal was to see whether by contemplating designs on cards, the "symbols" given by the Cabala, he could impose the designs upon another imagination. As he says in his autobiography, the experiments were remarkably successful.

Why did Yeats conduct these bizarre experiments? In part, he was trying to understand his own creative self. But beyond this he was still searching for a dynamic and imaginative background of belief for both himself and Ireland. Nineteenth-century Roman Catholicism and Protestantism alike seemed to have lost their power to inspire people to greater self-knowledge. It is a measure of Yeats's enthusiasm that through his cabalistic experiments he sought to found a new way of belief, one that would convince people of the power of the imagination. The sense of his own vocation comes through in a poem he addressed "To Ireland in the Coming Times," in 1892, most specifically in the following lines:

> *Because, to him who ponders well,*
> *My rhymes more than their rhyming tell*

> *Of things discovered in the deep,*
> *Where only body's laid asleep.*

But Yeats was soon to discover that religions are not made so easily. His mind was troubled by a confused welter of images that seemed to lead nowhere, and he declared himself adrift upon "the path of the chameleon."

The Order of the Golden Dawn expelled Mathers and some other errant members in 1900 and re-formed itself. Yeats figured prominently in the internal reform and the subsequent renaming of the Society as the Stella Matutina ("Morning Star").

In 1892 Yeats's second book of verse, *The Countess Kathleen and Various Legends and Lyrics,* was published.

"The Countess Kathleen" is a verse play. The narrative tells of an Irish countess who sells her soul to the Devil so that the peasants on her land will be saved from famine. It is a well-written little piece, simple and direct with an occasional moment of passion. Once again the reader becomes aware of Yeats's growing control over the medium of language.

The shorter poems in the volume are also a striking advance over Yeats's previous lyrics. Many of them are built around the symbol of the Rose. What does the Rose mean? It is difficult to say. Indeed, it is precisely because it stands for so many meanings that it becomes so successful a symbol. Yeats believed there is a principle of Ideal Beauty present in all human beings. Artists create

their art, and men and women learn to love each other
because of the presence of this principle. But the beauty
of art, or the beauty of the beloved, always falls
short of that beauty which can only be imagined. To
be in the service of Ideal Beauty is therefore a sorrowful
task, for the beauty one experiences in life always falls
short of the ideal. For Yeats the symbol of this Ideal
Beauty was the Eternal Rose. Sometimes the Rose is
embodied as a beautiful woman, as in the following lines
from "The Rose of the World":

> Who dreamed that beauty passes like a dream?
> For these red lips, with all their mournful pride,
> Mournful that no new wonder may betide,
> Troy passed away in one high funeral gleam,
> And Usna's children died.

Sometimes Yeats does not specify what the Rose stands
for; it almost becomes one of the symbolic designs of the
Cabala:

> *Red Rose, proud Rose, sad Rose of all my days!*
> *Come near me, while I sing the ancient ways:*
>
> .   .   .
>
> *Come near, that no more blinded by man's fate,*
> *I find under the boughs of love and hate,*
> *In all poor foolish things that live a day,*
> *Eternal beauty wandering on her way.*
>
> .   .   .

> *Come near; I would, before my time to go,*
> *Sing of old Eire and the ancient ways:*
> *Red Rose, proud Rose, sad Rose of all my days.*

> —"To the Rose Upon the Rood
> of Time"

Sometimes it is a small but significant ornament on the hem of Ireland's dress:

> *Because the red-rose-bordered hem*
> *Of her, whose history began*
> *Before God made the angelic clan,*
> *Trails all about the written page.*

> —"To Ireland in the Coming
> Times"

Yeats himself tells us that the idea of a principle of Ideal Beauty far superior to all human or natural beauty originally came to him through his old friends Spenser and Shelley. A Pre-Raphaelite, such as Dante Gabriel Rossetti, might also have contributed something. But the idea that this principle, although beyond human attainment, actually manifests itself in order that men and women may love and create beautiful things, Yeats felt, was his very own.

As for the Rose itself, Yeats tells us that the symbol is commonly used to represent Ireland. It is right that the poet does not give us more of a clue, for he is now writing poetry good enough to reveal its meaning to an

attentive reader. The discovery of this central and co-
hesive symbol gave Yeats's poetry a new maturity. In
his own words, in the poems addressed to the Rose, "he
has found, he believes, the only pathway whereon he
can hope to see with his own eyes the Eternal Rose of
Beauty and of Peace."

In spite of all these new strengths, the poems addressed
to the Rose seem a little out of touch with reality, too
dreamlike, too esoteric. Some poems in this second book,
however, show that when Yeats speaks in detail of his
beloved Irish countryside, a very real vividness results.
The most famous is "The Lake Isle of Innisfree" [pro-
nounced *In-nish-free*], composed while walking down
busy Fleet Street in London in a fit of anguished longing
for Sligo. The poem begins,

> I will arise and go now, and go to Innisfree,
> And a small cabin build there,
>   of clay and wattles made:
> Nine bean-rows will I have there,
>   a hive for the honeybee,
> And live alone in the bee-loud glade.

Another memorable poem is "The Man Who Dreamed
of Faeryland." Perhaps Yeats dramatizes his own predicament here, for the poem does have a curious immediacy. It tells of a man who could not participate in
life fully because he constantly dreamed of a place of
everlasting joy, love, and beauty. Earlier, in "The Wanderings of Oisin," the hero experiences a similar conflict,

torn as he is between a mortal life of human and heroic action on the one hand, and the enchantment of immortal joy, love, and beauty on the other. Clearly the predicament affected Yeats's imagination deeply.

Another important influence upon Yeats at this formative time was the work of the English poet William Blake. In his early life Blake had written some short poems of extraordinary surface simplicity, with an equally extraordinary complexity of symbolic meaning. Later, he had written vast, intricate, and utterly fantastic prophetic poems. Some sixty years had passed since Blake's death, and as yet no proper edition with an interpretation of these later poems had been made. In 1889 with Edwin J. Ellis, one of his father's rather eccentric friends, as collaborator, Yeats began such a work. The undertaking involved deciphering many manuscript pages in Blake's crabbed handwriting. The result was an illuminating and sound edition of Blake's works in three volumes that was published in 1893. Yeats's extensive critical introduction shows not only his understanding of Blake, but also gives indications of the overwhelming influence Blake's poetry was to have on him. In a sense the influence was so strong that it took a long time to ripen, and it is really only in Yeats's later poetry that one begins to feel the presence of Blake.

But at least one poem in *The Countess Kathleen* and *Various Legends and Lyrics* has a distinctly Blakean ring—"The Two Trees." The slightly odd and emphatic picture Yeats gives us of a tree growing inside a heart reminds the reader of Blake. There is also a Blakean refusal on the poet's part to explain the significance of the trees. Although he describes the trees very carefully, what they stand for remains enigmatic, is a puzzle left for the reader to solve. The poem, with its direct and forceful style—"Beloved, gaze in thine own heart, / The holy tree is growing there"—stands out in sharp contrast to the shadowy, dreamy style of the earlier Yeats.

In 1893 Yeats published another book, a little collection of stories called *The Celtic Twilight*, which opened with a short poem, "The Moods." The poem is noteworthy simply because it states one of Yeats's aesthetic theories of the time. The theory is a modification of what his father had told him earlier: in art and literature the only thing of value, the only lasting thing, is the expression of moments of heightened emotion. Yeats called such moments "moods"—in this case "fire-born moods" —and maintained through a paradox that they are the only permanent thing in this changing world:

> Time drops in decay,
> Like a candle burnt out,
> And the mountains and woods
> Have their day, have their day;
> What one in the rout
> Of the fire-born moods
> Has fallen away?

The stories themselves are beautiful cameos, tales and legends that Yeats had often heard from the West Irish country people. The limpid graceful prose shows again that when writing on Irish legend and folk lore, Yeats's style can be both vivid and beautifully simple. The purpose of the book is best described in Yeats's own words: "I have desired, like every artist, to create a little world out of the beautiful, pleasant, and significant things of this marred and clumsy world, and to show in a vision something of the face of Ireland to any of my own people who would look where I bid them."

Contemporary French literature was a very powerful force upon experimental British literature in the 1890's. It was mandatory for every young writer to make a pilgrimage to Paris. Yeats had already been introduced to the musical and suggestive French poetry of the French Symbolist school, and in 1894 and again in 1896, he went to Paris.

There he led the life of a typical young writer. He tried hashish; he went to the opening of *Ubu Roi*, the shocking new play by Alfred Jarry; he made the acquaintance of the poet Paul Verlaine. He also met the young Irish writer John M. Synge. Synge aspired to write on French matters and to follow European fashions in writing; Yeats characteristically advised him to go to Ireland for his material.

No account of these years in Yeats's life is complete without the story of his love for Maud Gonne, for the force of this passion lasted the rest of his life. She became a central symbol in most of his later poetry.

She was the magnificently beautiful daughter of an Irish father and an English mother. Yeats was first introduced to her at his father's house in 1889, and he immediately fell deeply in love with her. She was twenty-three and he was twenty-four at the time. She had been brought up to mingle in fashionable upper-class society, but, spurning that life, she had committed herself absolutely to the cause of Irish nationalism. Perhaps a little because she was a beautiful young woman with many romantic notions, but certainly also for many genuine political convictions, she believed in total activism of a cloak-and-dagger sort, and at the time Yeats met her, she was engaged in enlisting support for Ireland's cause. She was, of course, quite impatient with Yeats's belief in gradual change, in the importance of literature in the struggle for independence. She was a rabble-rouser, and in the passionate political speeches she made in Ireland and in France, she transfixed crowds as much by her fiery ardor as by her great beauty. All through the 1890's, she refused Yeats's repeated proposals of marriage, and the shadow of this hopeless love affair fell across his poetry. If the love poems of Yeats's second book of poetry seem to have a ring of urgency, it is certainly because of his feelings for her. No doubt he is able to express a convincing longing for the ideal Rose because he knows what real longing is like:

And then you came with those red mournful lips,
And with you came the whole of the world's tears,

> And all the sorrows or her labouring ships,
> And all burden of her myriad years.

—"The Sorrow of Love"

After half a decade of this passionate and unrequited love, Yeats seemed on the verge of some emotional relief. During a period of separation from Maud Gonne, and perhaps in some despair, he formed a relationship with a charming witty minor novelist, Olivia Shakespear. They even planned an elopement. But his near adoration for Maud Gonne destroyed his relationship with Mrs. Shakespear, who simply remained a lifelong friend and confidante.

Yeats's years from twenty-two to thirty-one, then, passed in extraordinary turbulence: creative work, Irish politics, London literary life, the occult, and love. His mind was wracked with the pursuit of ghostly images and of his unattainable love. He felt himself coming to a dead end. As he was taking his friend Arthur Symons around Ireland in 1896, a great wave of depression seemed to engulf him. They were staying at Tulira Castle, the residence of their friend Edward Martyn, a somewhat eccentric self-styled recluse who worshiped beauty in the fashion of Walter Pater. One afternoon Lady Augusta Gregory, a neighboring gentlewoman in her middle forties, drove up to invite Martyn's mother and the three friends to lunch. With that encounter, Yeats later said, the first act in the drama of his life came to an end.

CHAPTER 3

Years of Transition

IN THE next two decades of his life, Yeats changed profoundly. He began his thirties as a young man slowly exhausting himself in difficult pursuits. At fifty he was an established writer. Without the support of Lady Gregory he might not have been able to move smoothly through this important change. And it began at that visit to Edward Martyn's.

During their trip Yeats and Symons stayed at Coole House, Lady Gregory's residence. Seeing the young and gifted Yeats in such depression, she realized he needed rest and care, and at her invitation, he visited Coole for two months in the summer of 1897. He was to spend many of the following summers there, and would see her often in London during the year. In her, Yeats found the perfect patron.

Augusta Perss came from an old line of Anglo-Irish gentry. From her youth she had loved literature and the arts; and, what was then less usual, had a genuine interest in, and contact with, the Irish peasants of her native Galway. At twenty-seven she had married a career diplomat much older than she, who had taken her to the great European metropolises, and to the outer reaches of the British Empire in the Far East. This had given a cosmopolitan breadth to a character already rich in depth. When Yeats met her she was recently widowed and about forty-five years of age. She had already acquired a small reputation as a woman of letters, and had taught herself an impressive amount of Gaelic. She had always been close to the Galway peasantry and poor, and was well acquainted with original folk material. In 1893, at least two years before she met Yeats, she had read his collection of essays, *The Celtic Twilight*, and Douglas Hyde's *The Love Songs of Connacht*, a collection of Gaelic verse with accompanying prose translations. These books had inspired her to begin her own studies of Irish folklore. With her deep sympathy for Ireland and her international experience, she understood Yeats well.

Coole House was a large, rectangular, eighteenth-century building. Coole Park—the estate around the house —included a two-mile circular drive, woods, and a large lake full of swans. When Yeats first came to Coole, he was unable to find much beauty in the house and the park.

But "in later years I was to know the edges of that lake better than any spot on earth," and he came to love the extensive grounds, and the gaunt house, too, which was filled with the relics of a family active in imperial affairs. This change of heart reflected a deeper change in Yeats's outlook.

He had spent long years on a tight purse and amidst the petty squabbles that seem always to accompany political activity. He was slowly coming to realize that the gap between his noble ideals for Ireland and everyday realities was very wide indeed. One of the chief reasons for this, he began to suspect, was the rancorous personality and lack of taste of the so-called urban Irishman. Yeats never lost his faith in the simple virtues of the Irish peasantry, but he was looking for nation-building virtues, and through his association with Lady Gregory, he found these virtues among the members of the Anglo-Irish aristocracy. The Catholic native Irish, he felt, had no other country but Ireland to love. The pro-Irish Anglo-Irish might have cast in their lot more profitably with England, but had instead actively chosen to love Ireland and had given their talents to form a peculiarly Irish civilization.

Yeats's very gradual change of heart must be understood in all its humanness. On the simplest level it seems as if he is selling out to the class that oppressed and denied the native Irish. Certainly Maud Gonne thought so, and as we shall later see, Yeats himself had many misgivings about his new allegiance. But, as a poet whose faith was tied up with the expression of the individual self, he had deep-seated reasons for being disaffected with the ugliness of collective action and what it did to that individual self. To find in a group such as the Anglo-Irish in Ireland so many examples of individual virtue impressed him. Also, as a poet he had an extraordinarily heightened sensitivity to beauty. At Coole House he had a daily intimate experience with the beauty of an ordered, ceremonious way of life, and it so happened, this experience took place among intellectually active people. And no doubt the sheer grateful joy of relief from financial worries and exhaustion worked some of the change in him at first. At any rate, as readers of Yeats we have reason to be thankful for the change: it led to Yeats's activities in organizing a theatre and a transformation of his shadowy early Romantic verse into a tough resilient style.

Among the memorable people he met at Lady Gregory's house were her son Robert, a boy of fifteen when Yeats first met him, and her two nephews Hugh Lane and John Shawe-Taylor. Robert was especially gifted—handsome, gravely courteous yet on occasion lively, a good student of classics with real intellectual interests, a painter of promise, a splendid horseman and athlete. Hugh Lane was a wealthy art collector who had a positive commitment to educating public taste. Of John Shawe-Taylor, Yeats wrote in 1911: "I do not think I have ever known another man whose motives were so entirely pure, so entirely unmixed with any personal calculation, whether of ambition, of prudence or of vanity. He caught up into his imagination the public gain as other men their private gain." Shawe-Taylor worked hard to change the pernicious landholding system by bringing landowners and tenant farmers together in friendly bargaining sessions. In the Ireland of that time, this was indeed a revolutionary step.

Trying to find historical justification for his new appreciation of the Anglo-Irish aristocracy, Yeats discovered the eighteenth century in Ireland. During that century, he found, a handful of great Anglo-Irishmen of international stature had formed a solid, thoughtful, and constructive cultural core. Earlier, through his poetry and plays, as well as through his part in the literary movement, he had striven to make it possible for Ireland to recognize her legendary pagan roots. Now he wanted to extol the virtues that the Protestant eighteenth century had stood for at its best, most vividly represented by four men: Jonathan Swift, George Berkeley, Edmund Burke, and Henry Grattan.

But Yeats was slow to discover the Anglo-Irish eighteenth century. Before we consider that discovery and its effects, we shall turn to his life and work during the third decade of his life. These years still carry the impression of the early Yeats, while they also look forward to the new Yeats. They are, in other words, transitional years.

The significant work of the transitional years is some short stories, a book of poems, and five plays.

The Secret Rose, his book of short stories, was published in April 1897. As the title makes clear, Yeats is still working with the symbol of the Rose. Although not all the stories actually use the Rose, the concept of Ideal Beauty is pervasive throughout the book. Solitary artists and lovers are usually the central characters of the stories—a strange bird-king in "The Wisdom of the King"; lonely wanderers in "The Crucifixion of the Outcast" and in "Where There is Nothing, There is God"; a fanatical lover in "Of Costello the Proud." But the quintessential artist-lover of the collection is Red Hanrahan. Eight of the sixteen stories in the book are about him.

In Red Hanrahan Yeats combines the theme of the foredoomed pursuit of Ideal Beauty with the theme of the magic lure. Red Hanrahan is a poor "hedge schoolmaster," a wandering teacher whose home and classroom are under any roadside hedge. A common figure in Ireland at this time, the hedge schoolmaster was often the only source of education for the children of the Catholic peasantry. In a vision Sidhe (pronounced *shee*, fairies who are reputed to ride the whirlwind) appear to Red Hanrahan and make him their slave. He finds in himself the gift of poetry, but he is frightened by his vision because he senses that he is totally in the power of the Sidhe and that he is now so unlike other men that there is no place for him in society. Haunted, he wanders from place to place; finally he dies in a dream-vision, on top of the magic mountain Echtge. There he is mourned by a woman who is supposed to be mad, Whinny O'Byrne, whose lament seems to indicate that she is one of the Immortal Sidhe, Ideal Beauty come

down into the world to "make men mad." At the moment of Hanrahan's death,

faint white arms, wrought as of glistening cloud, came out of
the mud-stiffened tatters and were clasped about his body;
and a voice that sounded faint and far, but was of a marvel-
lous distinctness, whispered in his ears:—"You will seek me
no longer upon the breasts of women."

"Who are you?" he murmured.

"I am of those," was the answer, "who dwell in the minds
of the crazy and the diseased and the dying, and you are
mine until the world is melted like wax. Look, they have
lighted our wedding tapers." And he saw that the air was
crowded with pale hands, and that each hand held a long
taper like a rushlight.

Whinny O'Byrne sat by the body until morning, and then
began begging from barony to barony again, her monotonous chant keeping to the beat of her wrinkled heels in the
clinging dust: "I am beautiful, I am beautiful; the birds in
the air, the moths under the leaves, the flies over the water
look at me; for they never saw any one as beautiful as I am.
I am young, I am young! Look at me, mountains! look at me,
perishing woods! for my body will gleam like the white
waters when you have been hurried away. You and the races
of men, and the races of the animals, and the races of the fish,
and the winged races are dropping, like a guttering candle;
but I laugh aloud, remembering my youth!"

—"The Death of Hanrahan"

Like all the prose in *The Secret Rose*, this passage
has the lyric quality of folk poetry. In this folkloric

ghost story, however, Yeats is once more expressing complex themes. In this particular scene, for example, the use of ambiguity as the story draws to a close raises questions in the reader's mind. Is Whinny O'Byrne really an immortal being or is that only her mad fancy? Is this death that is also a wedding an event full of symbolic meanings, or does the author simply want to picture a dying man's hallucinations? The open-endedness of these questions is functional. For through them we arrive at the basic self-doubtings of the writer, doubts that he has expressed over and over again in his first creative decade: Are the poet's sayings symbolic insights into the human psyche, or are they meaningless word jingles that push him toward a kind of eccentricity that might almost be called madness? One cannot be sure what aspect of his own personality Yeats was exploring in Red Hanrahan, but that the character was important to him comes through when, some thirty years later, Yeats pleads in anguish in "The Tower," one of his greatest poems:

> Go therefore; but leave Hanrahan,
> For I need all his mighty memories.

"Rosa Alchemica," the last story in the collection, shows a very different Yeats. The plot ostensibly deals with two approaches to alchemy, medieval forerunner of chemistry, the chief goal of which was to change baser metals into gold. The "I" of the story is fascinated by this archaic science, and realizes that the alchemists' true goal was to discover the secret of immortal life: "their doctrine was no merely chemical phantasy, but a philosophy they applied to the world. . . . They sought to fashion gold out of common metals merely as part of an universal transmutation of all things into some divine and imperishable substance." But the protagonist's interest in alchemy is somewhat clinical. He constructs out of his alchemical studies "a fanciful reverie [of] the transmutation of life into art," and tries to make the interior of his house as well as the details of his personal life full of artistic beauty.

Of course Yeats's basic admiration for William Morris underlies the conception of this hero. But even more strongly recognizable is the influence of the French Symbolists. Morris had wanted to integrate life and art; so too did Yeats in his political program for Ireland. But during these transitional years Yeats was toying with the philosophy of French Symbolist writers like Joris Karl Huysmans and Villiers de l'Isle-Adam who rejected the importance of everyday life and wrote of a life style that was as deliberate and indeed artificial as an overly delicate and elaborate work of art. One of the stylistic characteristics of this philosophy was an obsessive attention to ornate but seemingly unnecessary detail; another, a belief in the correspondence between colors and emotions. Here is a passage from "Rosa Alchemica" that shows both the philosophy and the style:

I had only to go to my bookshelf, where every book was bound in leather, stamped with intricate ornament, and of a carefully chosen colour: Shakespeare in the orange of the glory of the world, Dante in the dull red of his anger, Milton in the blue grey of his formal calm; and I could experience what I would of human passions without their bitterness and without satiety.

Even Yeats's favorite notion, that there is sorrow attendant upon the service of Ideal Beauty, is turned into the delicate boredom of the typical turn-of-the-century hero. We are not surprised to discover that the main character has been a student in Paris.

To the hero's door comes an old friend, Michael Robartes, whom he has not seen for a long time. Robartes asks him to join the Society of the Alchemical Rose. One cannot remain merely clinically "interested" in the pursuit of immortality, Michael Robartes tells him. This doctrine is as potent a mind-changer as any religion and should be seriously accepted as such.

Against his will, the hero is made to participate in an extremely powerful ritual dance. At the end of it he discovers that his partner is "one who was more or less than human, and who was drinking up my soul as an ox drinks up a wayside pool; and I fell, and darkness passed over me." He retires into a cautious Christian faith. The story ends with these words: "I carry the rosary about my neck, and when I hear, or seem to hear them [the ritual dancers], I press it to my heart and say: 'He [Satan] whose name is Legion is at our doors deceiving our hearts with beauty, and we have no trust but in Thee'; and then the war that rages within me at other times is still, and I am at peace."

This curious story is a kind of anti-*Oisin*. If in the poem, pagan heroism is given the last word, here in the story Christian piety is the winner. But, as we have noted, the poem deals chiefly with the conflict between heroic physical earthly life and the immortal life of spiritual beauty. In the story Yeats seems to have discovered a graver issue: the single-minded pursuit of beauty may lead the artist to withdraw from the world, as the hero did before his meeting with Robartes. Or such a pursuit may lead to delusions of tyrannical control over the minds of others, a control the twilight people in the dance seem to possess. In his characteristic way, Yeats does not present this argument plainly: he embodies it in a fantastic story. The pursuit of the alchemical Rose is shown to have its dangerous side.

Yet Yeats was fascinated by the lure of the occult and by the possibilities of expanding one's spiritual powers. And that potentially dangerous aspect within himself he dramatizes in the figure of Michael Robartes. (Robartes participates in two other stories Yeats wrote at this time, "The Tables of the Law" and "The Adoration of the Magi.") To use Yeats's own aesthetic language: he has given names to his two most prevalent "moods." For his bewildered victimized Irish self—Red Hanrahan; for his cunning adventurous cosmopolitan self—Michael Robartes.

Yeats's book of poems, *The Wind Among the Reeds*,

was published in 1899, two years after *The Secret Rose.*
It contained, the critics acclaimed, his best verse, and in
terms of what Yeats had so far written, they were certainly right.

Sixteen of the book's thirty-seven poems are spoken
by three named figures or *personae:* Red Hanrahan, Michael Robartes, and Aedh (pronounced *Ay*), and from
the kinds of poems Yeats assigned to each, three distinct
personalities emerge. The tones of the three groups of
poems differ significantly and show us how boldly Yeats is
experimenting with the dramatic expression of "moods."
(For reasons he did not specify, Yeats removed the
speakers' names from the titles of the poems seven years
later. Today we can still distinguish between the speakers, and thus the "moods," but we no longer have the
names.)

The Hanrahan and Robartes moods are consistent with
their namesakes in the prose stories. Hanrahan is the
peasant visionary who understands visions in a simple
way and who reacts to them with naïve hopes and fears.
Expressive of Hanrahan's hopes is a beautiful little poem
now called, "The Song of Wandering Aengus." Here
Yeats uses traditional Irish symbols, such as the hazel
twig standing for wisdom. And he expresses a part of
one of his favorite themes, that the troubles in the poet's
mind lead him to long for immortality. But he has mastered the technique of expressing complex themes
through simple poetry so well by now that the poem
reads like a true folk song.

Robartes appears as a lover figure in *The Wind Among*

the Reeds. Just as he tries to convert the hero in "Rosa Alchemica," in these poems he tries to instruct his beloved. Do not be afraid of what I am trying to do with myself, he says; we shall come through.

As we would expect, his language is full of ornate imagery:

> When my arms wrap you round I press
> My heart upon the loveliness
> That has long faded from the world;
> The jewelled crowns that kings have hurled
> In shadowy pools, when armies fled;
> The love-tales wrought with silken thread
> By dreaming ladies upon cloth
> That has made fat the murderous moth. . . .
>
> —"He Remembers Forgotten
> Beauty" [earlier called
> "Michael Robartes Remembers
> Forgotten Beauty"]

Aedh, who appears as Aodh the minstrel in one of the minor prose stories, is the most extraordinary of the three figures. He is an extreme advocate of Yeats's theory of Ideal Beauty. If all the beautiful things in this world are destined to fall short of the principle of Ideal Beauty, it is best, Aedh the fanatic argues, that the beloved should die and enter the ideal realm. For then, as Beauty's priest, the lover can be truly united with his lady. It is only if we keep this argument in mind that a poem as enigmatic as the following becomes understandable:

Were you but lying cold and dead,
And lights were paling out of the West,
You would come hither, and bend your head,
And I would lay my head on your breast;
And you would murmur tender words,
Forgiving me, because you were dead. . . .

—"He Wishes His Beloved Were
Dead" [earlier called "Aedh
Wishes His Beloved Were
Dead"]

In another poem entitled "The Poet [earlier, Aedh]
Pleads with the Elemental Powers," he asks the mysterious powers of Nature and the human mind to restore
the Immortal Rose of Beauty to her heavenly home. Of
course, such a plea makes no sense in terms of ordinary
life. It is a mystic cry from a poet deeply troubled
by the thought that all beauty fades and dies—and only
the unending cycles of Nature and the commemorative
powers of the human creative imagination can keep the
Rose of Beauty "forever" alive.

Apart from the *persona* poems, perhaps the most remarkable poem in the book is "The Hosting of the
Sidhe." (In the summer of 1970, *The New Yorker* magazine reported, an Irish-American fireman in New York
City recited the poem and moved his hearers as much as
the readers of Yeats's day.) In sheer energy of movement, and in the immediate vividness given to an ancient
legend, the poem's achievement is masterful. In fact,
many of the poems in the book are addressed to the

Sidhe, "the everlasting voices," the ghostly inspirers of poetry. Noting that fact we can now make a generalization about Yeats's poetry: from the eighties to the end of the nineteenth century, Yeats dramatized the predicament of poetic inspiration in his verse and prose fantasies.

It is through his plays that Yeats most effectively sloughed off his earlier personality and developed his later one. To tell that story we must step back and consider once more the roots of Yeats's dissatisfaction with radical Irish politics.

In 1896 Yeats had joined the Irish Republican Brotherhood. Fully militant, this organization was committed to the cause of total independence from England at the cost of whatever violence might be necessary.

At the time of Yeats's joining, the Brotherhood was in the midst of organizing an immense anti-British demonstration in Dublin to take place in 1898. The occasion was to be the centenary celebration of the death of the Irish patriot Wolfe Tone. Tone had tried to enlist French military help against the British in Ireland in the 1790's, and Yeats and Maud Gonne were trying to take advantage of this fact of history by making arrangements to start a Young Ireland Society in France. Wolfe Tone had also had connections with the United States. He had emigrated there in 1796 and had received his introduction to French government circles through the French minister in Philadelphia. To take advantage of this connection, the enthusiastic and oratorical Maud Gonne wanted to go to America to work up American support for the Wolfe Tone centennial demonstration. While they were still in France, they received news that the Brotherhood had decided to withhold the funds necessary for her trip. This was a result of disunion between the London and Dublin members, who were not in agreement about the rights and wrongs of a political murder that had recently taken place in America.

Yeats had probably joined so militant a group as the Irish Republican Brotherhood because he wanted to please Maud Gonne. And now, primarily to find a way of acquiring the funds for the trip to America—though it is also true that Yeats was always ready to work against disunity—he maneuvered himself, in 1897, into being elected president of the Centennial Association, the steering committee for the demonstration.

Trying to bring the Dublin and London members together, Yeats was again embroiled in the kind of labor that had already brought him to the point of exhaustion two years ago. He had very noble plans. The Brotherhood would no longer tolerate the fact that Ireland had no Parliament of her own. The handful of Irish members in the British Parliament and the governance of Irish affairs through a viceroy from Britain constituted a reprehensible system. After extensive preparations, the Brotherhood would declare an independent Irish Parliament.

But the leaders of the Brotherhood had seen themselves too long as a militant group that thrived in an underground way with no prospect of major political victories. They were much more interested in their petty power plays within the group than in uniting drastically to constitute a nationally representative Parliament. Although the centennial celebrations had the demonstrations and speechmaking the Brotherhood hoped for, Yeats's long-range plans were largely ignored.

Yeats had never taken part so immediately in the politics of protest, and the involvement seems to have made it clear to him that he was unsuited for political work. His way of shaping Ireland's destiny must be through literature. Gradually he withdrew from direct political activity. Of course this meant the beginning of an estrangement from Maud Gonne. Although she had repeatedly refused to marry him, their lopsided comradeship had lasted. Certainly Yeats's adoration was as strong as ever. But she was an impulsive person, and felt that the calm, bountiful, intelligent, and motherly Lady Gregory was humoring and supporting Yeats's cowardly desire to disengage himself from his country's liberation.

Lady Gregory did sustain him during this critical period, a period during which the poet also lost his mother, long a confirmed invalid. As Yeats later chronicled in *Dramatis Personae*, now a section in his autobiography, "During those first years Lady Gregory was friend and hostess, a centre of peace, an adviser who never overestimated or underestimated trouble. . . ." She welcomed him to Coole and established a regimen for him: writing in moderation and, to relax the mind, field trips among the peasantry to gather folk tales. For the moment Yeats had had enough of politics. He enjoyed the intelligent sympathy of the high-born lady, and the simple authenticity of the peasant. Much later he was to write, "Lady Gregory, in her life much artifice, in her nature much pride, was born to see the glory of the world in a peasant mirror." Under the impetus of Yeats's friendship, Lady Gregory's own long-standing interest in the Irish past was quickened. She began to translate Gaelic myths. The result was books like *Cuchulain of Muirthemne, The Kiltartan Cross,* and *Gods and Fighting Men.*

For Yeats the means of forging Ireland's national consciousness would no longer be primarily poetry or fiction. He had come to feel more and more that there was no real reading public in Ireland. The experiments in translating books into Gaelic, writing original works in Gaelic, and spreading the learning of Gaelic made by Douglas Hyde's Gaelic League seemed to have created only coteries. Irish journalism, an inferior imitation of English partisan journalism, seemed to Yeats to be shallow and destructive. If a true and distinctively Irish drama could be created, it might reach many more people than poetry or fiction would, and might ignite the imagination as no newspaper could. As he said many years later in his address to the Swedish Royal Academy, "The great mass of our people, accustomed to interminable political speeches, read little, and so . . . we felt that we must have a theatre of our own." But, of course, such a project required money. It had been little more than a dream in Yeats's mind, to which he turned with great dedication when he left active politics.

In the summer of 1898, with the promise of money

from Lady Gregory and Edward Martyn, the dream came true. The Irish Literary Theatre, which was to become the Irish National Theatre and later the celebrated Abbey Theatre, was started. Its influence was quickly and centrally established on the Irish cultural scene, and the group continues to have a thriving existence.

The formal letter issued by the founders at the inception of the theatre is worth quoting from:

> We propose to have performed, in Dublin, in the spring of every year certain Celtic and Irish plays, which, whatever be their degree of excellence, will be written with a high ambition, and so build up a Celtic and Irish school of dramatic audience, trained to listen by its passion for oratory, and believe that our desire to bring upon the stage the deeper thoughts and emotions of Ireland will ensure for us a tolerant welcome, and that freedom to experiment which is not found in the theatres of England, and without which no new movement in art or literature can succeed. We will show that Ireland is not the home of buffoonery and of easy sentiment, as it has been represented, but the home of an ancient idealism. We are confident of the support of all Irish people. . . .

At first there were bureaucratic problems about getting a hall to play in. Lady Gregory exerted her influence, though, and the theatre was allowed to begin in the Antient Concert Rooms in Dublin.

In May 1899, the first show was given. Edward Martyn's *The Heather Field* and Yeats's verse play *The Countess Kathleen* were on the bill. Martyn was a pathologically devout Roman Catholic. Yeats's play—which,

as we have seen, showed an Irish countess selling her
soul to the Devil in order to save her people from
famine—was criticized by a monk as unchristian, more
specifically, anti-Catholic and anti-Irish. Martyn immediately decided to withdraw both his financial support
and his play, whereupon Yeats arranged for "two ecclesi-
astics" to read the play. They found nothing objection-
able in it, and Martyn was persuaded to return. When
The Countess Kathleen was performed, with Maud
Gonne in the title role, there was a disturbance in the
playhouse against the so-called irreligion of the play. This
beginning foreshadows the entire career of the Abbey
Theatre: clashes with popular opinion, fierce support
from a committed few, and a great sense of exhilaration
and creativity in the cause of patriotism among the man-
agers, actors, and playwrights.

John Synge, the young Irishman whom Yeats had first
met in Paris in 1896, joined forces with the company,
and showed himself to be a playwright of genius. Lady
Gregory began to write plays in Irish dialect, that beautiful and vigorous hybrid version of English spoken by
the native Irish in city and countryside. Yeats himself
wrote many plays for the group. Cuchulain, the semimythic Irish hero, became one of his major subjects.
From a scenario by Yeats, Douglas Hyde wrote the first
play ever written in Irish. For a time Yeats collaborated
in play-writing with the well-known novelist George
Moore, who was a cousin of Edward Martyn's. Their
two temperaments clashed in almost every way, and the

collaboration proved nearly fruitless. Their grotesque and tempestuous quarrels have become part of literary history.

After looking about for some time, and more often than not playing with British actors, the group of playwrights founded almost fortuitously a company of Irish players. Most of the actors performed not only because they loved acting but also because they loved Ireland, a fact that unified them with the playwrights. Among the actors, the Fay brothers, the Allgood sisters, and Florence Farr achieved extraordinary distinction and gave to the Abbey Theatre much of its famous early style. *The Shadowy Waters* and *On Baile's Strand* are representative of the five plays that Yeats wrote between 1896 and 1904.

The Shadowy Waters (1900) was apparently planned when Yeats was eighteen. The action takes place on a ship, and the play tells the story of a legendary king, Forgael, and Dectora, an alien queen captured by Forgael's sailors. The waters around the ship are indeed shadowy: often it is difficult to be sure of the nature of the action.

Forgael has much in common with Aedh. He is looking for a love that has none of the imperfections of a merely earthly passion:

> When I hold
> A woman in my arms, she sinks away
> As though the waters had flowed up between;
> And yet, there is a love that the gods give. . . .

Forgael's sailors are practical men. They want to rob a passing treasure ship and return home with their riches. The king wants to voyage to the world's end.

Dectora tries to incite the sailors to desert Forgael and take her to her own country, where she will reward them. The sailors agree, but at that very moment, Forgael begins to play on his magic harp, which throws the sailors into confusion. And Dectora beings to dream. She loses all sense of time and space and realizes that she has been waiting for Forgael all her life. She asks him to make his life with her. But, using a peculiarly Aedh-like argument, he tells her that love is perfect and complete in death, rather than in life, and asks her to share this fate. The language has all the ornateness of the Symbolist style as Forgael incants the names of precious stones:

> The love of all under the light of the sun
> Is but brief longing, and deceiving hope,
> And bodily tenderness; but love is made
> Imperishable fire under the boughs
> Of chrysoberyl and beryl and chrysolite,
> And chrysoprase and ruby and sardonyx.

The sailors leave and Forgael and Dectora sail on toward a mysterious and unspecified "death," which seems merely a name for the transformation of common reality into a magical universe. At the end of the play "the harp begins to murmur of itself," and Forgael declares: "The harp-strings have begun to cry out to the eagles."

The cryptic quality of this last statement is an indication of how much Yeats had been influenced by the European Symbolist theatre. No detail seems to mean what it would at face value. All seems charged with mystic meaning. When Dectora avows her love for Forgael, he says that the god of love and his divine beloved have now found human vehicles. This sense that the gods participate in human acts contributed to the general air of mystery. Even the ending, where the lovers share the prospect of death rather than a plan for life together, reminds us strongly of the conclusion of the best-known Symbolist play of the period, Villiers de l'Isle-Adam's *Axel*. Yeats had seen the premiere of this play in Paris in 1896 and had called it one of his "sacred books."

The Shadowy Waters was first printed in 1900. It was then more a long narrative poem than a play. Yet Yeats was interested in giving it dramatic form. Perhaps because it was the product of so early an inspiration, he gave a great deal of energy to revising the work. As a result, *The Shadowy Waters* exists in many different versions. In 1907 he published a substantially new "Acting Version" of the play designed primarily for the stage, much of which was written in prose. My quotations are from the original version, published in 1900.

If *The Shadowy Waters* is significant because it shows Yeats's debt to the Symbolists, *On Baile's Strand* is significant because Cuchulain is its hero. Cuchulain is a semimythic warrior who belongs to the Ulster Red Branch cycle of Irish epics, one of the two major cycles of the legends of pre-Christian Ireland. He is among the most famous of the heroes of ancient Gaelic legend; Lady Gregory's first significant book was *Cuchulain of Muirthemne*, a collection of legendary stories about this hero's exploits. Yeats was drawn to him first because many legendary queens and fairywomen had loved Cuchulain; second because he was a solitary brooding man; and third because his life was shot through with misfortune. Yeats wrote many plays and poems around him, and it was especially the manner of Cuchulain's death that fascinated him. *On Baile's Strand* (1903) was Yeats's first attempt to dramatize the Cuchulain story.

The particular story, with heroes of different names, is found in the legends of many countries: a father mourns his own killing of his unknown son.

Cuchulain, away on a voyage of conquest, falls in love with a captive queen, giving her a son. Then he leaves her to go back to his own country. She brings up her son in the sole hope that he will kill Cuchulain, for she is angered at what seems his rejection of her, and being a warrior queen, she cannot forget the fact of her initial defeat at his hands. In the main action of the play, Cuchulain's young son arrives at the camp of the Red Branch King Conchubar (pronounced *Connor*). Cuchulain does not know the youth's identity, and the youth does not know that Cuchulain is his father. He only knows that his mother has sent him to challenge Cuchulain in individual combat. Cuchulain accepts the challenge at Conchubar's command, and, though the two men feel an instinctive love for one another, they fight, true to the warrior code. Father kills son, then maddened by grief, rushes into the sea. The play ends with the ghastly scene of the great warrior hacking at the waves, mistaking them for an army of enemies.

Although the action belongs to the legendary past, the play does not have that general air of vague dreaminess that characterized Yeats's earlier plays as well as *The Shadowy Waters* and Symbolist theatre in general. Watching the terse action unfold, one realizes that Yeats has relearned his dramaturgy in an actual theatre. At the very outset of the play, Cuchulain is characterized in bold strokes in the contrast Yeats sets up between him and the sedentary Conchubar. The action is anchored in characterization rather than in magical vision. Another Yeatsian innovation that adds much to the effectiveness of the play is the introduction of the characters of the Blind Man and the Fool. Yeats had shown figures from folk life in his plays before this, his knowledge of Irish country folk helping him in these portrayals. But in *On Baile's Strand* he takes the bold step of introducing and concluding the high tragic story with two absurd and farcical characters. At the beginning of the play the Blind Man explains the forthcoming events to the Fool:

[Conchubar] will sit up in this chair and he'll say: "Take the oath, Cuchulain. I bid you take the oath. Do as I tell you. What are your wits compared with mine, and what are your riches compared with mine? And what sons have you to pay

your debts and to put a stone over you when you die? Take
the oath, I tell you. Take a strong oath.

   Fool [*crumpling himself up and whining*] I will not. I'll
take no oath. I want my dinner.

After the fatal combat it is the Blind Man who says
in Cuchulain's presence, "It is his own son that he has
slain." It is the Fool who finally shouts, "The waves have
mastered him!" The poignancy is raised to the highest
pitch when, at the end of the play, with Cuchulain
drowning, the Blind Man says to the Fool: "There will
be nobody in the houses. Come this way; come quickly!
The ovens will be full. We will put our hands into the
ovens."

CHAPTER 4
The Public Man

IN FEBRUARY 1903, Maud Gonne married Major John MacBride, a member of what was to become an extremist revolutionary group, the Sinn Fein (a Gaelic term, pronounced *shin fane*, meaning "we ourselves"). It was a choice typical of her rather mercurial character. There was no particular spiritual or cultural affinity between Maud Gonne and Major MacBride. Nor was theirs a relationship of any long standing. It would appear that she married him on an impulse because he was ready to lay down his life for the cause of Irish nationalism. Did she think of Yeats? Only so much as to send him the news in a note. It was brought to him while he was standing on a public platform, about to begin a lecture. For a moment everything went blank. And then, so unexpectedly, and so much in midstream, a new stage in his life began.

Yeats had paid single allegiance to Maud Gonne for nearly fifteen years. She had always turned down his proposals of marriage. They gave to one another a sort of impatient affection, she despising his moderate ideas, he deploring her political vehemence. Socially there were real differences between them. Yeats had grown up in the classless society of artists and intellectuals, Maud Gonne among the cosmopolitan British upper class. Their relationship rose above those differences. He had pulled her into the Theosophists' circle and the psychic experimentations of the Order of the Golden Dawn. She had tried to push him into political militancy. She was a woman often besieged by the loneliness brought on by great beauty, and in those moments Yeats had given her abundant sympathy. They had spent much time together, never as lovers. He, with a mixture of pity and adoration, had kept alive his hope for marriage. Now she had chosen a man totally unlike himself, a military man with a red moustache. It was not to be endured!

But the human mind somehow takes care of itself. In Yeats's case two things helped: the theatre and his poetic imagination.

In 1904, the theatre company he and Lady Gregory and Edward Martyn had organized was lucky enough to get a building of its own, the gift of Miss Annie E. F. Horniman. She was a wealthy Englishwoman who was deeply interested in supporting repertory theatre in Britain. In 1894 she had partly financed the performance of Yeats's first play, *The Land of Heart's Desire*, at the Avenue Theatre in London. She admired Yeats's work so much that, in order to give him free time, she had helped him with his correspondence for nearly five years. Now she presented the Irish National Theatre with a theatre in Dublin and an annual subsidy. The theatre was christened the Abbey Theatre because of its location on Abbey Street. It is a sad fact that Miss Horniman's part in the life of the Abbey Theatre quickly dwindled and finally came to an end. The company was too involved with the question of Irish identity to brook what they saw as an Englishwoman's interference.

Yeats threw himself into the running of the Abbey Theatre. *Samhain*, a journal that Yeats had established as the organ of the Irish Literary Theatre, shows the development of his theory of drama. Between 1897 and 1903, the years that we have called transitional, his primary concern was how to make the theatre (rather than the more remote forms of poetry and fiction) represent the true voice of the Irish people. Although that concern never disappeared, the emphasis changed as the century advanced. Here are some aspects of Yeats's new concerns.

He saw the Abbey Theatre as fully opposed to British and European commercial theatre—the theatre of frivolity and the theatre of social teaching. The British stage was beset by flippant plays of intrigue and romantic love set against a background of upper-class snobbery. The serious European stage, under the influence of the Norwegian playwright Ibsen, was occupied with plays discussing social problems, set against backgrounds so minutely realistic that the stage seemed a room with the fourth wall removed.

The frivolity of the British stage Yeats dismissed with contempt. Against realistic drama his charge was that the spirit of the audience would not be fundamentally moved if the spectacle on the stage seemed but a slice of life. Following the German poet Goethe, Yeats asserted that art was art precisely because it was not Nature. Rather than pretend that the play was real life, the dramatist should make the audience feel that what they were seeing was fictive. The spectator's imagination must not be lulled by a semblance of real life. He must make an imaginative effort to accept a play that is as seemingly unreal as religious ritual.

One way to ensure that the audience made this imaginative effort was to choose a subject that was simple, legendary, and fabulous. Another way was to use poetry or poetic prose as the medium of the play. Yeats had always been concerned with the musical enunciation of language. Now in his plays he constantly tried to make sure that dramatic speech came close to the condition of music. To make his plays deliberately fictive, Yeats also reduced the scenery to a symbolic one. Instead of backdrop and stage furniture imitating real life, he often used decorative designs on panels. Instead of the characters wearing costumes authentically reproducing the dress of the appropriate period, they wore flowing artistic robes of vibrant colors. Of course Yeats's early Pre-Raphaelite predilections were at work here. But Yeats was also moving with some of the most advanced thinking in contemporary British art theatre. Some of his scenes were designed by illustrious men of the theatre like Edmund Dulac and Gordon Craig.

His contacts with experimental techniques of production, as well as his father's early advice, made him conceive of acting itself in a new way. If the audience was to find moments of spiritual ecstasy in the playhouse, the play must reveal such moments of ecstasy. The actors must not smother those moments in fast-moving realistic acting. The pace must be slow, helping the audience to concentrate. The movements of the actors must be kept to a minimum, so that words and emotions could show their power.

From notions of a popular folk theatre Yeats is moving toward notions of a remote, refined, poetic drama that is nearly as solemn as ritual. The atmosphere of the stage is changing from rustic to decorative and esoteric. It is part of the change in Yeats's views that we have pointed toward in the last chapter. Of the seven plays that Yeats wrote during this period *The Hour-Glass* (1914) well shows this movement toward a dramatic practice that presents a very spare spectacle, the bare bones of a play, as it were.

In *The Hour-Glass* the central action of the play is utterly spare and intellectual. A wise man has taught all the people of the countryside the rationalistic doctrine that nothing exists that we cannot perceive through our senses. An angel announces to him that he must die when all the sand in the hour-glass has dropped to the bottom —in an hour—if he cannot find a person who believes in the existence of the supernatural. In a frenzy the wise man questions everyone. But all have learned their lessons too thoroughly. At last Teigue the Fool enters, the only person who has escaped the effects of the wise man's teaching. At first Teigue refuses to speak. When at last he agrees to talk, the wise man's final moment has come. In a miraculous move the wise man decides to accept the responsibility for his life's work, acknowledge his lifelong error, and stop the Fool from saying the saving words. Surrendering to God's will, he dies.

As we can see, the theme reflects a constant concern of Yeats's: the shortcomings of strict rationalism. Teigue the Fool, who sees visions of angels on a high hilltop, puts us in mind of Red Hanrahan. And there is a legendary Irish air about the play. It is not in the reiteration of these familiar aspects, but in the conception of the action itself that Yeats's new style can be seen.

None of Yeats's fascination with legend, love, or country life appears in the plot. How uncompromisingly theoretical the play is may be seen in these crucial lines, where the intellectual's difficulty in attaining faith is expressed through the encounter of Angel and Wise Man:

ANGEL.   Only when all the world has testified,
May soul confound it, crying out in joy,
And laughing on its lonely precipice.

What's dearth and death and sickness to the soul
That knows no virtue but itself? Nor could it,
So trembling with delight and mother-naked,
Live unabashed if the arguing world stood by.

WISE MAN.   It is as hard for you to understand
Why we have doubted as it is for us
To banish doubt. . . .

The play is built around the development of a single
passionate emotion—the wise man's anguish culminating
in an ecstasy of surrender to God's will:

It is enough, I know what fixed the station
Of star and cloud.
And knowing all, I cry
That whatso God has willed
On the instant be fulfilled,
Though that be my damnation. . . .

Working with the volatile Abbey Theatre group, reading and writing many plays, trying to give shape to his
ideas of a national theatre, and coping with all the details of mounting Abbey productions, Yeats was again
exhausting himself. His energies were all but depleted.
That he threw himself almost compulsively into this
enervating round of tasks is well described in a poem
published in 1910, "The Fascination of What's Difficult."
The central image of the poem is "our colt" Pegasus, the
winged horse of Greek mythology that lived on the

divine mountain Olympus. Pegasus was later associated with the poetic imagination, and this association is clearly present in Yeats's poem. The harshness of the verse describing Pegasus—"as though it dragged road-metal"—expressed the strain which the poetic imagination, accustomed to the heights of inspiration, must bear when forced into the labor of leading a national theatre:

> The fascination of what's difficult
> Has dried the sap out of my veins, and rent
> Spontaneous joy and natural content
> Out of my heart. There's some thing ails our colt
> That must, as if it had not holy blood,
> Nor on Olympus leaped from cloud to cloud,
> Shiver under the lash, strain, sweat, and jolt
> As though it dragged road-metal. My curse on plays
> That have to be set up in fifty ways,
> On the day's war with every knave and dolt,
> Theatre business, management of men.
> I swear before the dawn comes round again
> I'll find the stable and pull out the bolt.

Forcing his imagination into the unfamiliar and laborious channel of theatre business was one way, then, of coping with the loss of Maud Gonne. Another was the writing of poetry itself.

From the start Yeats had conceived of his life as material for poetry. Now his imagination began to convert the disaster of Maud Gonne's marriage into a mythical pattern. It was Homer's destiny to sing of Helen, Dante's to sing of Beatrice. So it was that he must sing of Maud. She was no longer a mere woman, but was transformed in Yeats's poems into the very spirit of poetry. Although the situation finally became so generalized that it is unnecessary for us to ask, Is this Maud Gonne who appears in the poem? certainly during this middle period of the poet's life, the immediacy of the pain has not been overcome:

> Others because you did not keep
> That deep-sworn vow have been friends of mine;
> Yet always when I look death in the face,
> When I clamber to the heights of sleep,
> Or when I grow excited with wine,
> Suddenly I meet your face.

> —"A Deep-Sworn Vow"

The urgency of the pain makes Yeats cry out in the direct language of passion, not in the indirect language of symbolism and mythology. In fact, the first instance of this use of direct, often conversational language is found in "Adam's Curse," a poem that was actually written a few months before Maud Gonne's marriage. It is a poem of melancholy rather than pain, although its language seems a rehearsal for the direct speech Yeats will use to express his impending loss. The poem is addressed to Maud Gonne and built around an actual incident. The directness of the style becomes evident immediately:

> We sat together at one summer's end,
> That beautiful mild woman, your close friend,
> And you and I, and talked of poetry. . . .

Poets work hard, though the fact must not be apparent in their work, Yeats the poet tells the others. The "beautiful mild woman" then replies:

> Although they do not talk of it at school—
> . . . we must labour to be beautiful.

It *is* an argument from an unrealistic world. But the direct language of lament for lost youth—Yeats and Maud Gonne were both thirty-seven at the time of the poem's writing—breaks through in the last stanza of the poem:

> I had a thought for no one's but your ears;
> That you were beautiful and that I strove
> To love you in the old high way of love;
> That it had all seemed happy, and yet we'd grown
> As weary-hearted as that hollow moon.

The poem appears in *In the Seven Woods*, a small book of verse Yeats brought out in 1903. It is in his next volume of poetry, *The Green Helmet and Other Poems* (1910) that we notice Yeats's mythicizing imagination turning personal loss into a Homeric theme. The most celebrated pair of such poems is "A Woman Homer

Sung" and "No Second Troy." The first poem ends in
this way:

> For she had fiery blood
> When I was young,
> And trod so sweetly proud
> As 'twere upon a cloud,
> A woman Homer sung,
> That life and letters seem
> But an heroic dream.

And the second, again comparing her to Helen of
Troy, the most celebrated beauty of the Greek legends,
runs:

> Why should I blame her that she filled my days
> With misery, or that she would of late
> Have taught to ignorant men most violent ways,
>
> .   .   .
>
> What could have made her peaceful with a mind
> That nobleness made simple as a fire,
> With beauty like a tightened bow, a kind
> That is not natural in an age like this,
> Being high and solitary and most stern?
> Why, what could she have done being what she is?
> Was there another Troy for her to burn?

Yeats had by now moved away from Irish political
life, centered in Dublin. Since the late 90's he had had

rooms in Woburn Buildings in London, where he lived when he was not at Coole or on strictly theatre business in Dublin. Here, between 1903 (when Maud Gonne married) and 1917 (when he himself married), he lived the apparently sociable and even somewhat influential life of an increasingly famous writer.

Lady Gregory took him to Italy in 1907. The Italy he saw was not a twentieth-century country, but a land of beautiful architecture, with buildings many centuries old. It was the bygone age of the Italian Renaissance that he experienced during his first Italian visit.

The Renaissance was an extraordinary explosion of cultural energy in Western Europe in the fourteenth, fifteenth, and sixteenth centuries. Italy was where it had begun. Among the many branches of learning and the arts that flourished under the impetus of the Renaissance, perhaps the most innovative was the cultivation of the art of living itself that was practised by Italian intellectuals and aristocrats who called themselves "humanists." Yeats had since youth been attracted by the ideal of a life that was beautiful in all its aspects. He had seen traces of such a life at Coole House. Traveling through Italy, stopping to see the splendid remains of the Renaissance architecture, he was reminded once again of the possibilities of beauty within an individual life—the possibilities of building within one's self resources of dignity, sweetness, and courtesy that expressed themselves through a well-tempered, learned, and active life. A book written during the Renaissance—Baldesar Castiglione's *The Courtier*—seemed to express this ideal most clearly to him. Perhaps, too, he was able to establish an imaginative relationship with Italy's past because he was traveling with Lady Gregory—for in the Renaissance, artists had been particularly fortunate in finding munificent patrons.

He visited Florence and saw the great cathedral dome designed by the fifteenth-century architect Brunelleschi. He visited the sixteenth-century city of Ferrara and reveled in its brick and terra-cotta palaces. He visited Ravenna in eastern Italy, where the works of art took him back a thousand years before the Renaissance. For Ravenna has monuments dating back to the fifth century, when it had been a Roman port trading with Asian countries like Turkey. Not surprisingly, the world-famous golden mosaics of Ravenna show a blending of Eastern and Western influences. Yeats was so moved by one of these mosaics—of the Apostles standing in a row —that twenty years later, in his poem "Sailing to Byzantium," he addressed this prayer to the memory of it: "O sages standing in God's holy fire / As in the gold mosaic of a wall, / Come from the holy fire, . . . / And be the singing masters of my soul."

But perhaps on this trip he was most struck by Urbino. The old city of Urbino, medieval in its outlines, is cut off from the main road, an isolated spot. The very countryside around it seems to belong to a more heroic age than ours. In it stands the noble fifteenth-century ducal palace, which was the scene of Castiglione's book. The spiritual excitement of Yeats's Italian journey is caught by the tone of this passage in his prose work *Discoveries* (1907):

The other day I was walking towards Urbino, . . . having crossed the Appenines from San Sepolcro, and had come to a level place on the mountain-top near the journey's end. . . . I was alone amid a visionary, fantastic, impossible scenery. It was sunset and the stormy clouds hung upon mountain after mountain, and far off on one great summit a cloud darker than the rest glimmered with lightning. Away south upon another mountain a mediaeval tower, with no building near nor any sign of life, rose into the clouds. I saw suddenly in the mind's eye an old man, erect and a little gaunt, standing in the door of the tower, while about him broke a windy light. He was the poet who had at last, because he had done so much for the word's sake, come to share in the dignity of the saint.

At the end of 1908 Yeats's stature as a writer became evident when the handsome *Collected Works* of *William B. Yeats* in eight volumes was issued by A. H. Bullen. Yeats accepted a seat on the Academic Committee of the English Royal Society of Literature. In 1911, he came to the United States on the first American tour of the Abbey Theatre and lectured with success.

In this and the previous chapter we have been working toward certain generalizations about what is going to be Yeats's mature middle style, in life as well as in poetry: a certain love for the introspective, even ritualistic virtues of a ceremonious way of life; an admiration for the Anglo-Irish eighteenth century; the acquiring of the voice of real passion; a tendency to convert the events of life into myth. But the catalogue is not complete.

Another entry in the catalogue must be Yeats's new reproving voice.

Through politics, literary coteries, and occultism, Yeats had dealt with people in groups before this. Now, however, he was a man in his forties with some measure of literary fame. His health was good. The tension of uncertainty over Maud Gonne was released. His early part in shaping Ireland's popular poetry and fiction, and his later part in shaping her drama, had not been inconsiderable; although his ideals had sometimes been foiled by popular apathy and journalistic malice, there had come about through his leadership a real change in the outlook and the standards of excellence of Irish writers. All these circumstances, added to his now first-hand knowledge of the language of drama, contributed to this new poetic stance: the bitterly oratorical public poet reprimanding a recalcitrant people—a far cry from the mystic poet finding a language for his dreams.

The reproving attitude was also strengthened by some controversies with which Yeats was associated at this time, one of them was the riot over Synge's play *The Playboy of the Western World* (1907).

This work is not only a masterpiece of the Irish theatre but a masterpiece of world drama. In it a fugitive Irish peasant boy Christy Mahon wins the sympathy and admiration of an entire village by telling the inhabitants how, unable to bear the taunts and insults of his father longer, he turned upon the old man and killed him in a fit of passion. Through scenes of incredible comic gusto and superb dialogue, Christy's exploit is recounted, and he is hailed as "the Playboy of the Western World." But suddenly Christy's irate father appears on the scene. It seems he had been stunned, not killed, by the blow. Goaded by fresh taunts and disgraced in the eyes of the villagers, Christy, for a moment cowed, pursues his father in a rage, and this time does indeed seem to kill him. The villlagers are attempting to turn him in to the police, when the elder Mahon, still not slain, enters on all fours. All this violent action has given Christy a new manhood, an ability to assert his power over his father. At the end of the play, he leaves the stage with these words: "I'll go romancing through a romping lifetime from this hour to the dawning of the Judgment Day."

The play is not a condonement of crime or violence. It is rather a loving presentation of the sheer joy in living that animates the Irish peasantry among all the adversities and wretchedness of life. And beyond the specifically Irish theme, the play touches universal themes: the creative power of the imagination, and the moment of initiation when a boy becomes a man.

Yet the insensitive Dublin public and Yeats's former friends the Irish nationalists found the play unpatriotic and lacking in all sympathy for the rural Irish. One excuse for the riot was the word "shift," used in the play in the sense of a woman's chemise. As a result of this animosity, the Abbey Theatre was the scene of wild disorder, and as Yeats has written, "on the last night there were, I believe, five hundred police keeping order in the theatre and its neighborhood." Both Yeats and his father spoke to the hostile audience from the stage. Yeats felt a bitter contempt for the petty unintelligent cruelty of the urban public and the nationalists. In a powerful and harsh poem written some years later, he compared their jealousy for genius to the jealousy of eunuchs for the sexual potency of Don Juan:

> *On Those That Hated*
> *"The Playboy of the Western World,"* *1907*

> Once when midnight smote the air,
> Eunuchs ran through Hell and met
> On every crowded street to stare
> Upon great Juan riding by:
> Even like these to rail and sweat
> Staring upon his sinewy thigh.

Another event that strengthened Yeats's reproving stance was the Hugh Lane controversy. Lady Gregory's nephew, Sir Hugh Lane, felt that the collection of modern French paintings which he had given to the city of Dublin should be housed properly, in a building designed by the famous architect Sir Edward Lutyens. A rich philanthropist offered to put up half the money for the building, if only the corporation of the city of Dublin would put up the other half. The public contribution was not forthcoming. There were disputes about design, location, and expenditure. Finally Lane sent the pictures to the National Gallery in London.

Yeats's mood of general bitterness is particularly evident in his protest against both the public's insensitivity to art, an insensitivity that affects the imaginative life of generations, and the rich man's unwillingness to give enough money to support art. In one poem, addressing the ghost of a great Irish patriot, he invokes Hugh Lane's history:

> A man
> Of your own passionate serving kind
> who had brought
> In his full hands what, had they only known,
> Had given their children's children
> loftier thought,
> Sweeter emotion, working in their veins
> Like gentle blood, has been driven from the place,
> And insult heaped upon him for his pains,
> And for his open-handedness, disgrace;
> Your enemy, an old foul mouth, had set
> The pack upon him.
>
> —"To a Shade"

In another poem he compares the insufficiently bountiful modern patron of the arts to the great Italian Renaissance patrons Duke Ercole I of Ferrara and Cosimo de' Medici, who had not waited upon public contributions. (The representatives of the Irish public are given common Irish peasant names—Paudeen and Biddy.)

> You gave, but will not give again
> Until enough of Paudeen's pence
> By Biddy's halfpennies have lain
> To be "some sort of evidence,"

. . .

What cared Duke Ercole, that bid
His mummers to the market-place,
What th' onion-sellers thought or did
So that his Plautus set the pace
For the Italian comedies?

. . .

And when they drove out Cosimo,
Indifferent how the rancour ran,
He gave the hours that they had set free
To Michelozzo's latest plan
For the San Marco Library,
Whence turbulent Italy should draw
Delight in Art whose end is peace, . . .

> —"To A Wealthy Man Who
> Promised a Second
> Subscription to the Dublin
> Municipal Gallery If It Were
> Proved the People Wanted
> Pictures"

These poems—the one on the *Playboy* riots and the two on the Hugh Lane controversy—were published in Yeats's 1914 book of poems, *Responsibilities.*

It was a startling book. As the title itself indicates, the poet is therein prepared to declare and accept his responsibilities to the world. He accepts the responsibility of his ancestry, even though it is Protestant and Anglo-Irish rather than Catholic and wholly Irish. He invokes his forefathers in the epigraphic poem: *"Merchant and*

scholar who have left me blood | That has not passed
through any huckster's loin, | Soldiers that gave, what-
ever die was cast.*" He accepts the responsibility for the
folly of his failed love. *"Pardon that for a barren passion's sake,"* the same poem continues, *"Although I have
come close on forty-nine, | I have no child, I have
nothing but a book, | Nothing but that to prove your
blood and mine.*" In this starkly autobiographical mood,
he also accepts the responsibility for a stark style—a new
"naked" style which is a deliberate renunciation of the
earlier "embroidered" one:

A Coat

> I made my song a coat
> Covered with embroideries
> Out of old mythologies
> From heel to throat;
> But the fools caught it,
> Wore it in the world's eyes
> As though they'd wrought it.
> Song, let them take it,
> For there's more enterprise
> In walking naked.

As he gives up the earlier rhythmical, songlike voice,
the lines sometimes spill over one into the other. Strong
pauses happen in irregular places. It is as if the rhythms
of conversation or unstructured thought are invading the
rhythms of song:

Indignant at the fumbling wits, the obscure spite
Of our old Paudeen in his shop, I stumbled blind
Among the stones and thorn-trees,
      under morning light;
Until a curlew cried and in the luminous wind
A curlew answered;
      and suddenly thereupon I thought
That on the lonely height where all are in God's eye,
There cannot be, confusion of our sound forgot,
A single soul that lacks a sweet crystalline cry.

—"Paudeen"

Sometimes he constructs a rough, almost crude fantasy quite unlike the shadowy romantic fantasy of the earlier Yeats:

Three old hermits took the air
By a cold and desolate sea,
First was muttering a prayer,
Second rummaged for a flea;
On a windy stone, the third,
Giddy with his hundredth year,
Sang unnoticed like a bird: . . .

—"The Three Hermits"

Certainly these poems involve the reader in a world of passionate personal urgency. "The Magi," one of the most accomplished poems in the book, is a good example. It has a subject that might well have been found in *The*

Wind Among the Reeds: the speaker sees visions of the
Wise Men who are unable to understand the apparent
ignominy of Christ's death. But whereas in the earlier
book, the subject would have been presented in the
languid, ornate, magical style of the Symbolist mode,
here it is presented as the hallucinatory obsession of a
very real speaker. Unelaborate adjectives like "stiff,"
"painted," and "rain-beaten" bring to the ancient event
the reality of something actually seen. The unvaried
repetition of "all" conveys the burdensome monotony
of an actual obsession. The contrastive and deliberately
clumsy collection of slightly odd, many-syllabled words
leaves a disturbing effect at the end of the poem (the
Nativity in the stable at Bethlehem becomes "the uncontrollable mystery on the bestial floor").

The Magi

Now as at all times I can see in the mind's eye,
In their stiff, painted clothes,
    the pale unsatisfied ones
Appear and disappear
    in the blue depth of the sky
With all their ancient faces
    like rain-beaten stones,
And all their helms of silver
    hovering side by side,
And all their eyes still fixed,
    hoping to find once more,
Being by Calvary's turbulence unsatisfied,
The uncontrollable mystery on the bestial floor.

The beginning of the First World War in 1914 did not move Yeats as much as we would expect. He had too recently emerged from the mire and violence of partisan politics. Also, he was too deeply involved in the question of Irish identity. He simply could not feel the reality of a war involving much of the Western world. The only two poems to come out of the war were personal ones, elegies for Lady Gregory's son, Robert, killed in action in the air over Italy. In fact, at the beginning of the war, when the expatriate American writer Henry James asked him for a war poem, he replied with this:

On Being Asked for a War Poem

I think it better that in times like these
A poet's mouth be silent, for in truth
We have no gift to set a statesman right;
He has had enough of meddling who can please
A young girl in the indolence of her youth,
Or an old man upon a winter's night.

A strangely dispassionate attitude! But the dispassion was severely shaken when on Easter Sunday 1916, the news arrived of an insane act of Irish heroism. Members of the Irish Republican Brotherhood occupied the General Post Office in Dublin. To hold out in that central public building in Ireland's capital city against British soldiery was a most significant and dangerous gesture, and, the Brotherhood hoped, would be a first step toward an uprising and the wrenching of power from the British. The men were, of course, finally captured; some of them were executed and some given long prison sentences. At first Yeats felt incredulous consternation at such a foolhardy act, then anguish because he was no longer a part of the bitter struggle in Ireland. The result was his first great political poem, "Easter 1916," whose final lines are almost a litany, chanting the names of the executed leaders, among them John MacBride, Maud Gonne's husband, who, estranged from Maud, had been living in obscurity:

> I write it out in a verse—
> MacDonagh and MacBride
> And Connolly and Pearse
> Now and in time to be,
> Wherever green is worn,
> Are changed, changed utterly:
> A terrible beauty is born.

In the theatre Yeats was in the middle of an experiment, an attempt to incorporate within English verse drama the conventions of the centuries-old, aristocratic Japanese Noh play. He had learned of this tradition from Ezra Pound, the expatriate American poet then living in England. Pound had introduced himself to Yeats in 1908. He was a person of high enthusiasm and obvious talent, and his personality soon charmed Yeats. He imparted to Yeats his views on writing and his adulation of the Far East. For three years Pound acted as Yeats's secretary; he looked after him in 1912 when the poet suffered violent and undignified bouts of indigestion; he read

aloud to Yeats, taught him how to fence. The wheel
seemed to have come full circle: William Butler Yeats,
himself once a young writer filled with revolutionary
ideas about his country's literature, was now "Big Bill"
(Pound's name for him), the picture of established success, being befriended by the next generation's youthful
prodigy. Dorothy Shakespear, whom Pound married in
1914, was the daughter of Yeats's old friend Olivia Shakespear, and this association with the Pounds fostered another relationship that Yeats came to value deeply: his
friendship with Georgie Hyde-Lees, Olivia's brother's
young stepniece, who became under Yeats's aegis a fellow
member of the Golden Dawn.

The Japanese Noh play seemed to contain answers to
Yeats's questions about the theatre: how to bring the
theatre close to the individual, how to avoid the dis-
tracting effects of naturalistic commercial theatre, how
to stir the deepest levels of the audience's consciousness.
The Noh seemed to emphasize with authority what
Yeats already felt: achieve distance from the events of
everyday life. If the playwright wishes to present "things
we feel and imagine in silence," rather than see and do in
active life, he cannot take the risk of making the events
on the stage appear too lifelike. The stage itself need
be no more than the intimate corner of a private sitting
room—a change, as it were, from symphony orchestra
to chamber-music group. The scenery in such a play
would be no more than a pair of beautiful folding screens.
The faces of the actors would be covered by elaborate
masks, so that facial expression would not remind us of

superficial emotions. The deepest passions, according to Noh principles, can be vividly portrayed by movements of the entire body. At the moment of climax there need be no emotional peak, only a dance. Yeats calls this new type of drama "indirect, distinguished, symbolic," and he discusses these discoveries in his essay "Certain Noble Plays of Japan."

The most obvious and direct result was his *Four Plays for Dancers:* "At the Hawk's Well" (1917), "The Only Jealousy of Emer" (1919), "The Dreaming of the Bones" (1919), and "Calvary" (1920). But the result of his work in what he understood to be the Noh tradition—the single dramatic moment revealed through music and dance, the actors distanced through masks—supported his own convictions about the nature of poetry and drama enough to color all his literary activity. He made Japanese friends—a Mr. Ito, "a traditional dancer of Japan," and later a Mr. Sato, a diplomat whose ceremonial sword Yeats would celebrate in his poem "Meditations in Time of Civil War." His encounter with the East was strengthened in 1912 by his meeting with Rabindranath Tagore, the Indian poet. Yeats looked over Tagore's English translation of the latter's volume of verse, *Gitanjali,* and was impressed enough to write an introduction to the book when it was published in 1912.

Yeats's earliest Noh play is "At the Hawk's Well," and as in *The Hour-Glass,* also a one-act play, the center of the drama is a single intense moment. But the action that surrounds that center has been pared down to a minimum, and it has been placed within a musical frame. The play opens ritualistically, with three musicians folding and unfolding a simple backdrop, a cloth with the design of a hawk, and chanting a song that describes the symbolic scene: a tree, a well, and the ghost-woman who guards the well. All through the play, the musicians remain on stage, accompanying the action with their instruments. At crucial points, they sing enigmatic questions that seem to indicate to the audience that the slow-moving action contains some meaning that reveals the deepest levels of the mind:

> "O wind, O salt wind, O sea wind!"
> Cries the heart, "it is time to sleep;
> Why wander and nothing to find?
> Better grow old and sleep."

An old man waits by the dry well. It is always dry and leaf-choked. At a certain miraculous instant, a little water splashes up in it. The old man has waited fifty years for the water, for to drink it is to receive immortality. The water has three times come to the well, but always at the important moment, he has fallen asleep.

Near the beginning of the play, Cuchulain enters. He, too, has come to seek the immortal waters. The moment is propitious. The ghostly hawk, to whom the well belongs, utters hawk cries through the voice of the guardian of the well, the ghost-woman. But once again the old man has fallen asleep. And Cuchulain, entranced, has followed the guardian offstage. Only the magicians are left onstage. First they speak:

> I have heard water plash, it comes, it comes;
> Look where it glitters. . . .

Then they sing:

> He has lost what may not be found
> Till men heap his burial-mound
> And all the history ends. . . .

Cuchulain and the old man reenter briefly. Yeats shows us that the elusive magic moment has passed. Cuchulain will resume his place in the world of battles and heroism; the old man will wait still more years for the water. The musicians end the play with two songs—an abstract philosophic one and a simple childlike one.

We have so far involved ourselves with Yeats's poetry and playwriting. Let us now cast a backward glance and catch up with the significant theoretical prose that he had also been producing, contained in the collections *Ideas of Good and Evil* (1903; this volume also contains some of his earlier writings), *The Cutting of an Agate* (1912), *Reveries over Childhood and Youth* (1915), and *Per Amica Silentia Lunae* (1917).

Among the essays in *Ideas of Good and Evil* are especially fine pieces on Shelley and Blake and a piece on the symbolism of poetry in which Yeats discusses his own theory of verse. But the most famous essay in the collection is "Magic," written as early as 1901. The essay opens with a credo:

> I believe . . . (1) That the borders of our mind are ever shifting, and that many minds can flow into one another, as it were, and create or reveal a single mind, a single energy.
>
> (2) That the borders of our memories are as shifting, and that our memories are a part of one great memory, the memory of Nature herself.
>
> (3) That this great mind and great memory can be evoked by symbols.

Although the title of Yeats's essay is "Magic," and it has its connections with the ancient occult lore that he had been studying since early youth, the beliefs that he asserts are, of course, not far from the speculations of respectable psychology. The first point allies itself with phenomena like telepathy and hypnosis. The second point is close to what C. G. Jung, one of the greatest psychological thinkers of the twentieth century, has suggested. But to us the third point is most interesting. It shows how much power Yeats assigned to the symbols he used. He believed that somewhere beyond its conscious everyday mind, mankind shares a great fundamental unity. This fundamental principle is what causes us to recognize and enjoy the meaningfulness of poetic symbols. Poetry thus has the function of unifying the deepest levels of human consciousness.

Yeats expresses these metaphysical speculations and this theory of poetry at much greater length in *Per Amica Silentia Lunae* (By the Friendly Silence of the Moon), a slim volume he published in 1917. In the fifteen years or so that passed between the publication of the essay and the beginning of his work on the book, Yeats had been arranging his thoughts about the nature of the soul and its relationship to the world.

Per Amica Silentia Lunae is divided into two parts—"Anima Hominis" (the soul of man) and "Anima Mundi" (the soul of the world). In the first part Yeats develops his metaphysical ideas. He sees the soul—or, as we would say today, the personality—of man as a struggle between two opposed elements, the self and the anti-self. The personality is always at odds with itself. The poet gives expression to this inevitable internal struggle. As Yeats puts it: "We make out of the quarrel with . . . ourselves, poetry."

In the second part of the book Yeats deals with the concept of the great universal spirit that the deepest levels of our individual spirits can touch, a concept he explored in "Magic." In trying to understand this concept, Yeats, like many great theologians and philosophers of the past, suggests that perhaps the memories and spirits of the dead continue life in a bodiless state until all the conflict within them is resolved. And perhaps the Anima Mundi, the soul of the world, is the habitation of these bodiless beings. Yeats was never quite sure of the factuality of this belief. But, as a poet who had felt that the images of his poetry came from an area outside himself, and as a late nineteenth-century man profoundly interested in spiritualism, he was fascinated by the very notion.

In the next period of his life, Yeats was to develop these speculations about the individual personality and the universal mind into an elaborate system.

Maud Gonne had been separated from Major Mac-Bride since 1905. For nearly a decade, she had lived with her adopted daughter Iseult, her son Séan, and a friend, Mrs. Clay, on the windswept coast of Normandy at Colleville, France. Yeats visited them from time to time and felt happy being accepted as a father-substitute by the two children. In 1916 John MacBride was executed as a result of the Easter Rising. Yeats, in Normandy that August, again proposed to Maud and was again refused. She refused him once more in the summer of 1917, and then, in a gesture at once pathetic, desperate, and slightly ridiculous, Yeats asked her lovely ethereal daughter to marry him. Iseult, who was very fond of him, refused him also, after a somewhat protracted period of girlish dalliance.

Maud Gonne had her heart set on returning to Ireland in time to campaign for the elections planned by the Irish Republicans in December 1918. Yet the British government in Ireland had issued a warrant for her arrest as soon as she should set foot on Irish soil. With trepidation Yeats accompanied her and Iseult to London. In London, the authorities forbade her to proceed to Ireland. To Yeats's great relief, she agreed to remain in

London for the time being. For Iseult he found a job as assistant librarian at the School of Oriental Languages.

Yeats went back to the friendship of the charming, witty, and intelligent George Hyde-Lees. He was fifty-two; she, twenty-six. She had been a loving and sympathetic friend for five years. Yeats had tried the generosity of her spirit sorely in the last few months. Now they came together again and were married on October 21, 1917. On their honeymoon she showed a capacity for writing with her conscious mind suspended—automatic writing, as it is called. This discovery was to lead Yeats into a labor of years. But that is the story of the next epoch of his life.

Painting of W. B. Yeats by
Augustus John, 1907
(*The Bettmann Archive*)

Two photographs of Yeats
as a young man
(*Brown Brothers*)

Ben Bulben Mountain, which
Yeats celebrates in his poems. It is
in the county of Sligo, where
he spent much of his childhood.
(Irish Tourist Board)

Lady Gregory at Coole Park,
her estate *(Irish Tourist Board)*

A tree at Coole Park on which visitors carved their initials. Yeats's can be seen in the center of the picture. *(Irish Tourist Board)*

The old Abbey Theatre in Dublin *(Irish Tourist Board)*

Yeats and his wife, George Hyde Lees, on a lecture tour of the United States in 1920 (*The Bettmann Archive*)

Yeats at the time of the same visit to America *(Culver Pictures)*

Below left, Thoor Ballylee in Gort, Ireland, the tower Yeats restored and lived in briefly with his wife and children. *Right,* an inscription on a stone at Thoor Ballylee *(Irish Tourist Board)*

I the poet William Yeats.
With old millboards and
    sea-green slates.
And smithy work from
    the Gort forge.
Restored this tower
    for my wife George.
And may these characters
    remain
When all is ruin once again.

Yeats in the later years *(Irish Tourist Board)*

Yeats and the poet T. S. Eliot
in 1932, at the time of
Yeats's third lecture tour of
America *(Pictorial Parade)*

The hotel in Roquebrune
in the south of France in
which Yeats died
(Reg Innell)

Yeats's grave in Drumcliff churchyard in Sligo, "Under bare Ben Bulben's head" (Irish Tourist Board)

The inscription on Yeats's tombstone (Irish Tourist Board)

CHAPTER 5

The Vision
Articulated

On the afternoon of October 24th 1917, four days after
my marriage, my wife surprised me by attempting automatic writing. What came in disjointed sentences, in
almost illegible writing, was so exciting, sometimes so
profound, that I persuaded her to give an hour or two
day after day to the unknown writer, and after some half-
dozen such hours offered to spend what remained of life
explaining and piecing together those scattered sentences.

—Introduction to *A Vision*

T HE NEXT decade in Yeats's life cen-
tered around "the explaining and piecing together" of a
systematic symbology. He had increasingly come to re-

alize that he was not only a poet of personal experience, and even a poet of social consciousness, but he was also a poet whose imagination tended toward philosophy. In these years Yeats began to establish new roots, both personal and philosophic.

The Yeatses spent two months in Oxford, and the greater part of 1918 and 1919 in Dublin. Yeats wanted his first child to be born in Ireland. At No. 73 Stephen's Green, a house owned by Maud Gonne, Anne Butler Yeats was born on February 24, 1919.

Dublin was full of violent political activity. The Easter Uprising in 1916 had given the people of Ireland an emotional rallying point. An Irish Parliament had been elected and had declared Ireland to be free from all British control. Yeats felt uneasy, out of place in all this fervor; he had set himself apart from Irish politics for too long. Ireland for him was now a private country, hidden in desolate places.

Yeats had always given symbolic form to his own life. He had constructed for himself, in turn, the roles of the committed young poet trying to restore to the common people an Irish self-image based on past glory, of the dreamer, the harsh public poet reproving the middle class, and the bard in the great tradition mourning the loss of an impossible love. With his marriage, his craving for an Ireland relating to his own private life, and his pursuit of his wife's "Unknown Instructors" (as he called the possible sources of her automatic writing), a new symbolic pattern entered his life. He had long admired

Milton and Shelley's image of a philosopher looking for wisdom in the top room of a tower. Now he imposed this image upon his own life; he bought from Lady Gregory a lonely, centuries-old, squat, square, battlemented tower (with cottage, garden, mill wheel, brook, and bridge attached) in Galway. He christened it Thoor (Gaelic for tower) Ballylee. It came to represent, in his poetry and thought, the proper dwelling of the poet.

The walls of the staircase were painted peacock blue. Mrs. Yeats devoted herself to the kitchen garden. Heavy beautiful oak furniture was made on the spot for the upper rooms. Even the fact that frequent Atlantic gales did not make feasible the kind of sea-green slate roof Yeats wanted became in his mind an indicator of symbolic truth: "Is every modern nation like the tower, half dead at the top?" Although the Yeatses did not live in the tower for very long, and finally had to abandon it altogether because of Yeats's ill-health, for himself and his readers the tower seemed symbolic of Yeats's poetry in the 1920's and 30's. The spirit of the enterprise is caught in this little poem:

To Be Carved on a Stone at Thoor Ballylee

I, the poet William Yeats,
With old mill boards and sea-green slates,
And smithy work from the Gort forge,
Restored this tower for my wife George;
And may these characters remain
When all is ruin once again.

Yeats paid for the restoration and furnishing of the tower from his considerable earnings from a third American lecture tour. He and his wife were in America in the early months of 1920. Yeats traveled to Pittsburgh, New York, Washington, New Haven, Salt Lake City, and other places. He read his own poetry in the peculiar musical monotone that had acquired power and authority by this time. He discussed the circumstances of the poems' composition. The tour was a great success.

In New York, Yeats saw his father again after a considerable period of time. John Butler Yeats had lived in New York since 1908. He had a small apartment in a residential hotel. He was still an active painter, but had become even more of a "personality." He and his son had always kept up a vigorous correspondence, exchanging thoughts in their old dynamic way, the son's voice getting stronger as the years passed. Yeats was pleased to see his father so comfortable. This was to be their last meeting. John Butler Yeats died on February 3, 1922.

From his American tour Yeats returned to Oxford. Dublin was too disquieting, and the tower was not yet fit for permanent residence. As a halfway move, he bought and settled in a house in Oxford. The atmosphere of the ancient university town pleased him. He loved Oxford's famous Bodleian Library and pursued his odd tastes in reading there. He found a following among literary and intellectual undergraduates who were welcome at his house. Once again we have the sense of the wheel turning full circle. Yeats, who had once sat at the feet of O'Leary, Henley, Morris, was now the one whose feet were being sat at. He thoroughly enjoyed the reversal of roles and even thought of making Oxford a center of Noh Theatre.

Life in Oxford was pleasant with the companionship of youth, wise age, and aristocracy. Yeats's participation in Oxford life was fairly active. He even spoke at the famed Oxford Union "against the terrorist policy of the British Government in Ireland." But the Irish poet longed for his own country.

Conditions in Ireland were full of potential violence. Ireland's parliamentary body, the Dáil Éireann (pronounced *Dhawíl Aire-ánn*) and the Irish Republican Army were of course not recognized by the British government, which was at the time in the hands of the Conservative Party. In 1921, the Dáil sent some representatives to the British Prime Minister, David Lloyd George, to negotiate the terms of a treaty between Ireland and Great Britain, whereby Ireland would gain her independence. Once in London the two chief members of the group found themselves faced with the threat of total war unless they agreed to sign a treaty that would, among other humiliating measures, divide Ireland in two, creating a pro-British Protestant enclave in the six counties of the North, put the Republican Army under English control and make every Irish national swear an oath of allegiance to the English crown. Under such a massive threat from a powerful country, the two Irish members signed the treaty and returned to Ireland. Especially among the Protestants of Northern Ireland and conservative elements in the country as a whole, there had always existed sentiments for a peaceful union with Britain. The treaty polarized Ireland very effectively. It drove a powerful wedge between this group and that large part of Ireland, where feeling against the English was solidly rooted. The republic itself was now divided into pro-treaty and anti-treaty factions. The seeds of civil war had been sown. All through the early twenties, the British took away power after power from the Dáil Éireann until in 1922 a Provisional Irish Government, nearly dictated by English authorities, in effect abolished the Dáil. Every step taken by the British and the pro-treaty Irish had been accompanied by fighting between Irishman and Irishman. Violence had erupted all over Ireland, but Dublin was its center.

Yeats hesitated to bring son (Michael, born in 1921), daughter, and wife into this charged atmosphere. Not for long, however. He bought a house in Merrion Square in Dublin, and moved into it in 1922. Trinity College honored him with a doctorate, and so did the University of Belfast.

"A furious civil war" broke out in April 1922, after the Irish Free State was established with English approval. Yeats and his family were then living in the tower at Ballylee. Just as at the time of the Easter Rising in 1916 Yeats had felt himself estranged from the center of action in Dublin, so also the civil war gave him a sense of being far from the action, not only physically but also in spirit. All through these years of literary success and the achievement of personal security, Yeats had moved ever farther away from the revolutionary spirit of his youth. But he had commemorated the Easter Rising of 1916 in his verse, and now once again he turned to poetry. The eloquent posture of "Meditations in Time of Civil War," as compared to the strained beauty of "Easter 1916," is a measure of the maturing of Yeats's poetic genius.

Although the center of the civil war was in Dublin, its impact was felt all over Ireland. The little bridge over Yeats's brook at Ballylee was blown up. Yeats himself has described the state of affairs at Ballylee:

> We are closed in, and the key is turned
> On our uncertainty; somewhere
> A man is killed, or a house burned,
> Yet no clear fact is to be discerned:
> Come build in the empty house of the stare.
>
> A barricade of stone or wood;
> Some fourteen days of civil war;
> Last night they trundled down the road
> That dead young soldier in his blood:
> Come build in the empty house of the stare.

> —"Meditations in Time of
> Civil War"

In January 1922 the Irish Free State had been established with English approval. Ireland now had a Parliament with two houses. Yeats's friend Oliver St. John Gogarty pressed Yeats's claim to a place in the upper house—the Senate—and Yeats was accordingly among the thirty senators chosen by President Cosgrave to represent "distinguished aspects of the nation's life."

Yeats was pleased with the appointment. From youth he had wanted a role in the making of Ireland, and this seemed an opportunity. He did not align himself with the men of letters in the Senate. He associated rather with businessmen, bankers, even military men, people who knew the practical world and could soberly and patiently "get things done." His speeches in the Senate, which have been collected in a book, show that he played his part with dignity and energy; but it must be admitted that he was not at the center of things.

His place in the Senate made one quiet but significant change in his life. Being a senator of the Irish Free State meant support of and collaboration with the English and thus a betrayal of the uncompromising spirit of the Irish Republican Brotherhood. He was now in full disgrace in the eyes of Maud Gonne.

In 1924 Yeats was awarded the Nobel Prize for Literature. It can properly be said that the award took him by surprise. In spite of all his elegance of manner and gravity of accomplishment, he had never lost the ability to be childishly pleased at good news. He went to Sweden for the awarding ceremony, which took place at the royal palace at Stockholm. The king himself presented the award. This was Yeats's first experience of a court. He has given a vivid account of his impressions, included in his autobiography, entitled "The Bounty of Sweden."

After a few days of appropriately regal celebration, he gave a lecture. There he spoke of himself largely as a dramatist, because he felt that public recognition of his name had come about because he had helped found a national theatre. He spoke of John Synge, dead fifteen years before, and of Lady Gregory, "a living woman sinking into the infirmity of age," and of the creative joy of their association.

Now that he was nearly sixty himself, his health began to weaken. In search of a pleasant and healthful climate, he and his wife went to Sicily at the end of 1924. He spent almost a year abroad, and his health improved. He spent some time in Rapallo with Ezra Pound. He read Italian and German philosophy. He was at work on the section of his autobiography entitled "Trembling of the Veil." He traveled at a relaxed pace, delighting in the beauties of Italian art and architecture, the gorgeous mosaic on the walls and floors.

In the spring he returned to Ballylee, to begin a period of incredible creative vigor.

At the end of 1925, he published the remarkable book called *A Vision*. This work of prose was the result of the long arranging of thought with which he had been occupied ever since his days at Coole Park. To his own thoughts he had added the vastly suggestive symbolic material received from those "unknown instructors" who seemed to control his wife's automatic writing. To understand those messages he had broadened his own readings in philosophy and history. All this had fermented in Yeats's mind, a mind that was neither scholarly nor systematic but gifted with an exuberant imagination. Once again, to put *Per Amica Silentia Lunae,* his earlier speculative work, beside *A Vision,* is to be astonished at Yeats's inner growth.

Yeats was not satisfied with the first published version of *A Vision.* He revised it very thoroughly, and a second edition was printed in 1937. As it stands, it incorporates his thoughts on the nature of reality and history.

Per Amica Silentia Lunae, as we have already seen had tried to relate the soul of man ("Anima Hominis") to the soul of the world ("Anima Mundi"). *A Vision* tries to relate five subjects: how man thinks, the varieties of human personality, life after death, how historical periods are determined, and the cultural history of Europe. The books falls into five main sections.

The first two sections are introductory, containing "A Packet for Ezra Pound" and "Stories of Michael Robartes and His Friends." In the first, Yeats gives us a description of the scene in Rapallo, Italy, where he completed the final revisions of the book; and tells us that *A Vision* is an explanation and amplification of the cryptic messages he received through his wife's automatic writing. In the second, he gives a fictitious account of the discovery of *A Vision,* supposedly a medieval document entitled *Speculum Angelorum et Hominum* (Mirror of Angels and Men). "Stories of Michael Robartes and His Friends" is a good example of Yeats's occultist playfulness. Robartes, the *persona* of the occultist, speculative, and daringly experimental side of Yeats's own personality that he devised as early as *The Wind Among the Reeds*, is given out to be the discoverer of the document—the wisdom of *A Vision*.

The third section presents two of Yeats's major concerns: how man thinks, and the varieties of human personality. It is contained in Books I and II of *A Vision*, called "The Great Wheel" and "The Completed Symbol."

In all his prose and in his autobiography, we can watch Yeats watching himself, trying to discover the precise way in which his mind works. In *Per Amica* he had made a systematic statement: man's thought is a constant pursuit of its own opposite. In "The Great Wheel," helped perhaps by Mrs. Yeats's unknown instructors, he consolidated that earlier statement. Any human thought, "every movement of the mind," as Yeats later put it, generates, while it continues on its own track, the opposite of that thought. Slowly the opposed thought gains ground, until it becomes so strong that it engulfs and destroys the original thought. In the meantime, however, the opposite of this second thought has been inevitably increasing, ready to overflow and engulf *it*. This process would continue for ever, but for the fact that thoughts are broken off artificially. The process (the technical term for it is *dialectical*) describes not only individual thoughts but all mental activity, even the long-drawn-out collections of thoughts represented by periods of intellectual history such as the Renaissance or the Enlightenment.

Yeats explains his next topic of interest—the varieties of human personality—with the help of this dialectical method. He recognizes two chief elements in all human character. One he calls "primary" or "objective"—an interest in things other than one's self. The second he calls "antithetical" or "subjective"—an interest in one's own self. There is a dialectical play of these two elements in all human character. But the amount of either element in a single personality may vary. Yeats plots a wheel upon which he places the different kinds of personality according to the amount of objectivity and subjectivity present in them. He isolates twenty-six different varieties. A purely subjective or a purely objective mind cannot belong to any human being. But to make his diagram complete, Yeats includes these two models of personality in his account as well. The part of his book where Yeats discusses the varieties of human personality —called "The Twenty-eight Incarnations"—is interesting because in it he comments on the creative personalities of many artists and great men and women. It is diverting, for example, to see, that he gives to Walt Whitman a highly "objective" personality, with the "subjective" impulses on the rise: "Walt Whitman makes catalogues of all that has moved him, or amused his eye, that he may grow more poetical." To Martin Luther, on the other hand, Yeats gives a personality with an excess of subjectivity that has the "objective" impulses on the rise: "Born as it seems to the arrogance of belief . . . [he] must reverse himself, . . . purify the intellect . . . till this intellect accepts some social order, some condition of life, some organised belief: the convictions of Christendom perhaps."

Before we pass on from this important second section, let us examine some of the key images employed in it, images that will also be used in many poems: the double cone, the Mask, and the phases of the moon.

The double cone is the diagrammatic figure that expresses the dialectical principle itself. One element, represented by one cone, grows bigger, while the other element, represented by the second cone, grows smaller. Since the dialectical play of a thing and its opposite— one increasing as the other diminishes, and vice versa—is unending, the figure of the double cone is in constant motion, the cones moving dialectically back and forth. The alternating movements in history and the alternating mixture of subjectivity and objectivity in human personality can thus be represented by the shuttling double cone. It looks like this:

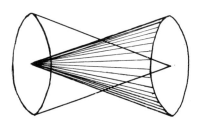

Yeats often calls this a "gyre," and likens its motion, for which he resurrected the archaic word *perne*, to that of a weaver's shuttle or bobbin.

"Perne" and "gyre," then, both indicate a spiraling

movement, the natural movement of history and of the human spirit. Yeats's poetry is full of spiral images—the winding (or unwinding) of the mummy's shroud, the winding staircase of the tower, and many others. Often in a poem when the speaker has a vision of immortal beings, such an image is assigned to those beings. Here are the two most celebrated examples, one from "The Wild Swans at Coole," and the other—a passage which we have already quoted in another context—from "Sailing to Byzantium." The significant words are italicized.

The first passage speaks of the wild swans and the speaker's attempt to count them:

> I saw, before I had well finished,
> All suddenly mount
> And scatter *wheeling in great broken rings*
> Upon their clamorous wings.

The second passage invokes the images of saints contained in a mosaic:

> O sages standing in God's holy fire
> As in the gold mosaic of a wall,
> Come from the holy fire, *perne in a gyre,*
> And be the singing-masters of my soul.

The Mask is a concept that Yeats had already introduced in *Per Amica Silentia Lunae.* A man desires to be exactly what he is not. This is part of his dialectical

nature. He often wills into being an image of himself
whose qualities are opposite to those originally possessed
by his native self. Sometimes he sees in the image of the
person he loves the presence of all those qualities. To
this image of himself or to the image of the beloved,
Yeats gives the name Mask. All the personality types of
"The Twenty-Eight Incarnations" are computed in terms
of the being's pursuit of the Mask.

The Phases of the Moon may be explained as follows.
Yeats found a natural symbol for the twenty-eight incarnations of the human personality in the twenty-eight
phases of the moon. As you know, the proportion of
darkness in the moon's face slowly decreases as it waxes
during the first fourteen nights of the lunar month, and
slowly increases as it wanes during the last fourteen.
This, Yeats believed, corresponded to the proportion of
"objectivity" in the succeeding personalities on the sche-
matic diagram of personalities. Therefore Yeats made
moonlight the sign for "subjectivity," and sunlight or
darkness (both opposites of moonlight) signs of "objectivity." The two impossible personalities were identified with the fifteenth phase of the moon, or the full
moon (complete subjectivity), and the first phase of the
moon, or the New Moon (complete objectivity). As
Yeats makes Michael Robartes say in one of the poems
he included in *A Vision:*

> Twenty-and-eight the phases of the moon,
> The full and the moon's dark and all the crescents,
> Twenty-and-eight, and yet but six-and-twenty

The cradles that a man must needs be rocked in:
For there's no human life at the full or the dark.

—"The Phases of the Moon"

Since the dialectical pattern describes all movements
of the mind, the phases of the moon, like the action of
the double cone, may be taken to represent not only the
types of human personality but the varying degrees of
"subjective-objective" mixture in a single human life as
well. In fact, if we examine the growth of the speaker
of Yeats's poems throughout his career, we begin to see
the presence of these stages. The insights of *A Vision*
are a consolidation of intuitions and thoughts he had been
turning over in his mind for many years.

Book III, called "The Soul in Judgment," and Book IV,
called "The Great Year of the Ancients," give us speculations on life after death and descriptions of how the
ancient mathematicians and philosophers computed the
cycles of the world's great ages.

The final section is perhaps the most fascinating in
the book. It is called "Dove or Swan" and in it Yeats
applies the diagrams of the double cone and the phases
of the moon to the cultural history of Europe. Here we
get the poet's vision of his own heritage, and it brings
us very close to his mature mind.

According to the nature of dialectical movement, as
the diagram of the double cone should explain, there is
a moment when the direction of forces must be reversed.

If we translate the concept of this moment into Yeats's understanding of European history, we must say there is a moment when a predominantly subjective period of history (with the objective principle increasing within it) changes into a predominantly objective period (with the subjective principle increasing within it). Yeats saw this moment of change as beyond human control and dependent upon a supernatural push. The moment is often symbolized by the begetting of a child by a god upon a mortal woman. Yeats gives us two such symbolic encounters: the god Zeus in the shape of a swan ravishing the young girl Leda and begetting Helen of Troy; and the begetting of Jesus on Mary by the Holy Ghost—traditionally represented as a dove. Thus the title "Dove or Swan" reflects Yeats's question about the present age. Will it resemble the predominantly subjective (with the objective on the rise) pre-Christian civilization, or will it imitate the predominantly objective (with the subjective on the rise) civilization of Christianity? This question is put in a characteristically veiled way at the end of *A Vision:* "Shall we follow the image of Heracles that walks through the darkness bow in hand, or mount to that other Heracles, man, not image, he that has for his bride Hebe, 'The daughter of Zeus, the mighty, and Hera, shod with gold'?" The close relationship between *A Vision* and Yeats's poetry reveals itself in the same question asked in the poem "The Second Coming." In a terrified mood, the poet imagines another Annunciation, like the Ledean and the Christian ones, in his own troubled time:

Surely some revelation is at hand;
Surely the Second Coming is at hand.
The Second Coming! Hardly are those words out
When a vast image out of *Spiritus Mundi*
Troubles my sight: somewhere in sands of the desert
A shape with lion body and the head of a man,
A gaze blank and pitiless as the sun,
Is moving its slow thighs, while all about it
Reel shadows of the indignant desert birds.
The darkness drops again; but now I know
That twenty centuries of stony sleep
Were vexed to nightmare by a rocking cradle,
And what rough beast, its hour come round at last,
Slouches towards Bethlehem to be born?

As in the case of human personality, so in history. The
conditions represented by the first and fifteenth phases
of the moon cannot exist. But especially the fifteenth
phase—the condition of the soul's greatest fulfillment—
tantalized Yeats's imagination, and in sixth-century Byzantium he found the cultural equivalent to the twelfth,
thirteenth, and fourteenth phases, the closest history
could come to the ideal fifteenth. Byzantium, today's
Istanbul, was the eastern seat of the Roman Empire and
the Christian Church. Before the fourth century, it had
been a Greek colony and one of the centers of trade
between Greece and the Near East. In the fourth century, the Roman Emperor Constantine the Great rebuilt
the city and renamed it Constantinople, making it his
capital as well as the seat of eastern Christianity. His

sixth-century successor, Justinian the Great, built the
magnificent church of St. Sophia, dedicated neither to God
nor saint but to Divine Wisdom herself. After Byzantium's
capture by the Turks in 1453, the city became the capital
of the Ottoman Empire and so remained until 1923.

Byzantium-Constantinople-Istanbul, a city embracing
three great cultures—Greek, Christian, Islamic—and
resplendent with brilliant architecture, seemed to Yeats
to have brought together the civilizations of the East
and West most successfully in the age of Justinian. In a
passage restating his youthful ideal of the Unity of Culture, he describes that glorious period in Byzantium:

> I think if I could be given a month of Antiquity and leave to
> spend it where I chose, I would spend it in Byzantium a
> little before Justinian opened St. Sophia and closed the
> Academy of Plato. I think I could find in some little wine-
> shop some philosophical worker in mosaic who could answer
> all my questions. . . . I think that in early Byzantium, maybe
> never before or since in recorded history, religious, aesthetic
> and practical life were one, that architect and artificers . . .
> spoke to the multitude and the few alike.

In his poetry Byzantium became the symbol of the heal-
ing power of art and the creative process.

Why did Yeats write such a peculiar book as *A Vision?*
Perhaps in part the unconscious minds of the poet and
his wife suggested this fantasy of symbols from the depths
of their lifelong occultist interests. But certainly the
book also reflects Yeats's genuine engrossment in ques-

tions of philosophy, psychology, the meaning of history. His training and preference did not lie in academic or purely intellectual speculation. With a poet's imagination and his fascination with mysterious systems of knowledge, he concocted this brilliant, poetic, and sometimes nearly incomprehensible book which contains much beautiful and discerning writing.

Having explored and written out on paper all the theory that had been active within him, Yeats felt a curious liberation, and during the twenties, he experienced a period of great creative vigor. The poems of this period were published in *The Tower* (1929). They are among the best and most influential poems written in this century.

Perhaps because of the energy he gave to the organizing of *A Vision* during these years, the voice he uses is the proud voice of the overreaching magician Michael Robartes:

> I pace upon the battlements and stare
> On the foundations of a house, or where
> Tree, like a sooty finger, starts from the earth;
> And send imagination forth
> Under the day's declining beam, and call
> Images and memories
> From ruin or from ancient trees,
> For I would ask a question of them all.

These lines are from "The Tower," the title poem of the book. The "battlements" and "foundations" are the actual battlements and foundations of Thoor Ballylee, and the landscape the actual landscape around it. In this volume Yeats tries to express his own relationship to the place of his residence and the condition of his country, and ultimately his relationship to history, in a most direct way. In "The Tower" itself, for example, he clarifies his relationship to history by writing an eloquent testament:

> It is time that I wrote my will;
> I choose upstanding men
> That climb the streams until
> The fountain leap, and at dawn
> Drop their cast at the side
> Of dripping stone; I declare
> They shall inherit my pride,
> The pride of people that were
> Bound neither to Cause nor to State,
> Neither to slaves that were spat on,
> Nor to the tyrants that spat,
> The people of Burke and of Grattan
> That gave, though free to refuse— . . .

After this moving tribute to the Anglo-Irish of the eighteenth century, his own people, he relates himself also to his wider European heritage:

I have prepared my peace
With learned Italian things
And the proud stones of Greece,
Poet's imaginings
And memories of love, . . .

The combination of the awareness of old age (Yeats is entering his sixties) and awareness of history is expressed also in "Meditations in Time of Civil War" (1923), "Nineteen Hundred and Nineteen" (1921), and "Among School Children" (1927).

In "Meditations in Time of Civil War" the opening relationship with history and tradition is established in the poet's initial choice of the old-fashioned, slow moving, alternately rhyming iambic pentameter line. In the opening lines, the poet presents the beauty of the gracious Anglo-Irish way of life. Notice how sharply the false rhyme of "mechanical/call" pulls us up by contrast to the mesmeric regularity of the verse and thus gives us a wordless sense that the seeds of strife might well be contained within this beautiful display of wealth and culture:

Surely among a rich man's flowering lawns,
Amid the rustle of his planted hills,
Life overflows without ambitious pains;
And rains down life until the basin spills,
And mounts more dizzy high the more it rains
As though to choose whatever shape it wills
And never stoop to a mechanical
Or servile shape, at others' beck and call.

The title of this first section of the poem is "Ancestral Houses." In the third section—"My Table"—the effect of *A Vision* is marked. Yeats is using a kind of occultist shorthand to describe a gift from his Japanese friend, Mr. Sato:

> Two heavy trestles, and a board
> Where Sato's gift, a changeless sword,
> By pen and paper lies,
> That it may moralise
> My days out of their aimlessness.
> A bit of an embroidered dress
> Covers its wooden sheath.
> Chaucer had not drawn breath
> When it was forged. In Sato's house,
> Curved like new moon, moon-luminous,
> It lay five hundred years.
> Yet if no change appears
> No moon; only an aching heart
> Conceives a changeless work of art.

If we have read *A Vision* carefully, we know that the poet is here aligning himself not only with the history of his own people but with the general history of the human spirit. And so the poem progresses through "My Descendants" (where the poet speaks of his two children), "The Road At My Door" (where he consoles himself for his uninvolvement in military action in Ireland), and "The Stare's Nest by My Window" (where he prays for symbolic regeneration, "Honey-bees, / Come build in the empty house of the stare"), until it arrives at the startling last section "I See Phantoms of Hatred and of the Heart's Fullness and of the Coming Emptiness." Here the themes of aging poet, turbulent Ireland, the establishment of a relationship with history, and occult visions merge. "I climb to the tower-top and lean upon broken stone," the section begins. "Under the light of a moon that seems unlike itself," the poet sees phantoms of hatred that seem to symbolize the fratricidal hatred that infects Ireland. The vision presents with shocking vividness a historical parallel, the violent persecution of the crusading Order of the Knights Templars in the fourteenth century and the murder of Jacques de Molay, their last Grand Master. This violent parallel is soothingly replaced by the soul's ideal of perfect subjectivity. Yeats constructs the serene scene in the complex symbological language of *A Vision* and of esoteric lore, and perhaps with memories of a sixteenth-century tapestry:

> Their legs long, delicate and slender,
>   aquamarine their eyes,
> Magical unicorns bear ladies on their backs.
> The ladies close their musing eyes. No prophecies,
> Remembered out of Babylonian almanacs,
> Have closed the ladies' eyes,
>   their minds are but a pool
> Where even longing drowns under its own excess;
> Nothing but stillness can remain
>   when hearts are full
> Of their own sweetness, bodies of their loveliness.

The drugged monotone of the "ess" words seems to reflect the speaker's wonder at the magic vision.

But reality intrudes upon this lovely stasis. "Brazen hawks" "have put out the moon." And the poet falls back upon the sedentary esoteric pursuits of his own old age: "The abstract joy, / The half-read wisdom of daemonic images, / Suffice the ageing man as once the growing boy."

But the combination—old age, esoteric philosophy, history, and visionary ending—is expressed most vividly in perhaps the greatest poem in *The Tower,* "Among School Children."

One of Yeats's public duties as senator was the inspection of schools. "Among School Children" opens with the poet sensing the incongruity of the situation of an old man as he walks into a classroom full of children, accompanied by a nun. He sees himself as concealing that incongruity under the mask of a "sixty-year-old smiling public man." As he watches the children, he begins to imagine Maud Gonne, "a Ledaean body," as a child. Since he had never known her as a child, that recollection is purely imaginary. Then her present sixty-year-old face, still beautiful but gaunt, "floats into the mind," and the poet relates it to history by seeing its similarity to the faces in the paintings and sculptures of fifteenth-century (Quattrocento) Italy:

> Did Quattrocento finger fashion it
> Hollow of cheek as though it drank the wind
> And took a mess of shadows for its meat?

Through the dark language of third-century Neoplaton-ism, his mind wanders to the futility of a mother's love for a child that will inevitably grow old and pitiful and the futility of the nuns' worship of religious images that "keep a marble or a bronze repose" and seem "self-born mockers of man's enterprise." On the way to this thought his mind pauses a moment on Pythagoras, Plato, Aristotle —the great triad of ancient Greek philosophers. Plato taught that the world of experience had no true reality; only the world of the spirit was real. Aristotle—Alexan-der the Great's tutor—taught that a thing's reality could be reached only by understanding its function, and there-fore as a philosopher Aristotle was "solider." Pytha-goras surmised that as the stars and planets moved in perfect rhythm they created an unearthly "music of the spheres." Yet all three men were subject to the laws of time, grew old and decrepit, and died. The verse where Yeats expresses this theme of inevitable mortality and presents these grand philosophies is a perfect example of the absolutely shocking yet flawless coarseness with which Yeats drives great thoughts into the reader's heart:

> Plato thought nature but a spume that plays
> Upon a ghostly paradigm of things;
> Solider Aristotle played the taws
> Upon the bottom of a king of kings;
> World-famous golden-thighed Pythagoras
> Fingered upon a fiddle-stick or strings
> What a star sang or careless Muses heard:
> Old clothes upon old sticks to scare a bird.

From the arrogant slipshod rhythm of "world-famous golden-thighed," "fiddlestick or strings" the language, halting for a stanza on a bemused working out of a supposed parallel between nuns and mothers, suddenly soars to the exquisite vision of perfect labor far beyond philosophers', nuns', or mothers' dreams, accessible perhaps only to the poet's imagination:

> Labour is blossoming or dancing where
> The body is not bruised to pleasure soul,
> Nor beauty born out of its own despair,
> Nor blear-eyed wisdom out of midnight oil.
> O chestnut-tree, great-rooted blossomer,
> Are you the leaf, the blossom or the bole?
> O body swayed to music, O brightening glance,
> How can we know the dancer from the dance?

Yeats drops that last effortless and memorable question coolly. Yet it is totally ambiguous, reflecting two opposed philosophies. Either, how can we know the reality of human beings apart from their actions? or, How can we possibly know the reality of human beings through their actions alone? The Yeats of this period is a master of the rhetorical question. One is reminded of the last lines of "Leda and the Swan," in which the poet wonders if the woman who is made the instrument of divine birth acquires any share of divine wisdom:

> Did she put on his knowledge with his power
> Before the indifferent beak had let her drop?

Throughout the 1920's, Yeats was deeply immersed in the theatre. He lectured to raise money for the Abbey Theatre and continued to write plays for it. His dramatic style, keeping pace with his poetry and his life style, had taken on an easy strength, a masterful humor.

The Player Queen (1922) is steeped in the theories of *A Vision*. The poet Septimus worships his wife Decima in his mask as a poet. He writes adoring verse to her. But he makes love to his mistress Nona in his everyday self as a man of flesh and blood, and a craftsman of poetry. He composes the poems "upon [her] shoulder. Ay, and down along [her] spine in the small hours of the morning; so many beats a line, and for every beat a tap of the fingers." It is a parable of the relationship between life and poetry. Septimus, Decima, and Nona are all part of a theatre company, which is performing for the queen the story of Noah and the Flood. As *A Vision* repeatedly insinuates, all life can be seen as a free-form play and obviously Yeats's plot has to do with a crucial turning point of the double-cone—the end of one era and the beginning of another. Decima has been given the part of Noah's wife, but she will not play it. She is hiding.

Meanwhile many of the supernatural signs associated with the end of an age have been seen by the simple local inhabitants. The one that frightens them most is that the chaste young orphan queen has been seen coupling with a unicorn in her high-walled garden. We recognize here one of Yeats's favorite symbols—the coupling of human and divine—Leda and the swan, Mary and the Holy Ghost. For the unicorn is a traditional as well as a Yeatsian symbol of divine chastity and non-violent power. As in "The Second Coming," Yeats seems to be saying, "Surely some revelation is at hand."

The queen is well known for her shyness and lack of elegance, whereas Decima the poet's wife is vivacious, immoral, and devastating. But at the end of an era one tendency gives way to and is replaced by its opposite. By a quick-change act that nobody in the cast but everybody in the audience is aware of, the real queen slips away to a convent and Decima—"the player queen"—ascends the throne.

Even from such a rough summary it seems clear that although the play has a strict theoretical underpinning, it is fast moving in its own right. But what cannot be captured by any summary is the comic gusto and the quick wit of the action and the dialogue. Not only does the theoretical burden of the play not encroach upon our pleasure, but we are entirely caught up in the play's dramatic presence. There is music, poetry, dance, and folk humor in the play's very fabric—it is sheer pageantry, as perhaps all successful symbolic theatre must be. The characterizations of the dupe-poet Septimus, the shy Queen Octema, the earthy Nona, and the arch Decima are inimitable.

The play ends with a dance of all the players dressed as animals for the pageant of Noah and the Flood. All the farce in the play has given way to a gripping solemnity. The new queen (Decima) hides her face behind the mask of Noah's wife. She is bidding good-bye to her previous actress self, and beginning to accept fully her new queenly self. She must tell her erstwhile fellow players to dismiss the old Decima from their minds. She makes the nonplussed Prime Minister summon the players. Here is her concluding speech to them:

> You are banished and must not return upon pain of death, and yet not one of you shall be poorer because banished. That I promise. But you have lost one thing that I will not restore. A woman player has left you. Do not mourn her. She was a bad, headstrong, cruel woman, and seeks destruction somewhere and with some man she knows nothing of; such a woman they tell me that this mask would well become, this foolish, smiling face! Come, dance.
>
> [*They dance, and at certain moments she cries* "Good-bye, good-bye" *or else* "Farewell." *And She throws them money.*]

The dance of the animals may be a symbol of the moment at the center of the spiral when one cone gives way to another. The whirling poise of the dance engaged Yeats's imagination as a symbol of that point when movement, about to change direction, has a moment of rest. We have noticed it at the end of "Among School Children."

Another play of this period, *The Cat and the Moon* (1928), is very spare, written in the tradition of the Japanese Noh. As is usual with the Noh, the play begins and ends with a song presented by onstage musicians. The protagonists are a Blind Beggar and a Lame Beggar. From *On Baile's Strand* we know that Yeats became interested in such characters through his knowledge of the Irish folk tradition. And so in *The Cat and the Moon* Yeats is once again strengthening native Irish writing by bringing it in touch with international strains. He innovates on the Noh tradition by making the First Musician a Holy Man, the saintly hero of the play. But Yeats writes nothing in this period that does not express the same concerns that went into *A Vision*. *The Cat and the Moon* has as its theme the same miraculous moment as *The Player Queen*. Yeats explains it thus in a note added to the play: "When the Saint mounts upon the back of the Lame Beggar he personifies a certain great spiritual event which may take place when Primary Tincture ["objectivity"] . . . supersedes Antithetical ["subjectivity"]." But to understand the beautiful comic clarity of the dramatic genius of Yeats at this period, one should compare this weighty explanation to the light touch at the end of the play, where the event actually takes place:

FIRST MUSICIAN.   You must dance.

LAME BEGGAR.   But how can I dance? Ain't I a lame man?

FIRST MUSICIAN.   Aren't you blessed?

LAME BEGGAR.   Maybe so.

FIRST MUSICIAN.   Aren't you a miracle?

LAME BEGGAR.   I am, Holy Man.

FIRST MUSICIAN.   Then dance, and that'll be a miracle.

[*The Lame Beggar begins to dance, at first clumsily, moving about with his stick, then he throws away the stick and dances more and more quickly. Whenever he strikes the ground strongly with his lame foot, the cymbals clash. He goes out dancing, after which follows the First Musician's song.*]

In October 1927, Yeats suffered from congestion of the lungs. The illness became so grave that Mrs. Yeats took him to Spain. It was a strange time. The poet was alarmingly ill, yet continued to write the most moving poetry, much of which was published in *The Winding Stair* (1929) and *Words for Music Perhaps* (1932).

Three methods of expression that Yeats had already experimented with come to a certain ripeness in these books of poetry. His vision of himself in history, especially the history of eighteenth-century Protestant Ireland, may be identified as the source of the first method. The great examples of it are "Blood and the Moon" and "Coole Park and Ballylee, 1931."

In "Blood and the Moon," Yeats reinforces his symbolic relationship to the tower. "Blessed be this place, / More blessed still this tower," the poem begins. He next declares that the greatest Irish cultural heroes of the eighteenth century—Jonathan Swift (Dean of Dublin's St. Patrick's Cathedral, and therefore "the Dean" in this

poem), Burke, Berkeley, Goldsmith—have climbed to
this tower top up the spiral staircase. We recognize the
symbol of all history—the gyre—in the image of that
spiral staircase. Yeats is identifying himself, as the
present owner of the tower, with the cultural forces of
the eighteenth century. The polysyllabic and difficult
energy of the verses makes them worth quoting:

> I declare this tower is my symbol; I declare
> This winding, gyring, spiring treadmill of a stair
>   is my ancestral stair;
> That Goldsmith and the Dean,
>   Berkeley and Burke have travelled there.

> Swift beating on his breast
>   in sibylline frenzy blind
> Because the heart in his blood-sodden breast
>   had dragged him down into mankind,
> Goldsmith deliberately sipping at the honey-pot
>   of his mind,

> And haughtier-headed Burke
>   that proved the State a tree,
> That this unconquerable labyrinth of the birds,
>   century after century,
> Cast but dead leaves to mathematical equality;

> And God-appointed Berkeley
>   that proved all things a dream,

That this pragmatical, preposterous pig of a world,
    its farrow that so solid seem,
Must vanish on the instant
    if the mind but change its theme;

.   .   .

The strength that gives our blood
    and state magnanimity of its own desire;
Everything that is not God
    consumed with intellectual fire.

In "Coole Park and Ballylee, 1931" the poet con-
templates the little stream that runs "under my window-
ledge." As befits the visionary poet, he sees in it an
emblem of the soul of man. Then he imagines the great
eighteenth-century domain of Lady Gregory's Coole. He
remembers himself standing by Coole Lake, and a swan
rising. "Another emblem there!" he exclaims, and gradually his mind turns to the old age of his dear friend
Augusta Gregory. It is as if she is the last representative
of a glorious and bountiful culture. From that thought
he turns to self-definition—his poetry seems to belong
to a more ceremonious past than to the fragmented and
tortured present:

Sound of a stick upon the floor, a sound
From somebody that toils from chair to chair;
Beloved books that famous hands have bound,
Old marble heads, old pictures everywhere;

.   .   .

A spot whereon the founders lived and died
Seemed once more dear than life; ancestral trees,
Or gardens rich in memory glorified
Marriages, alliances and families,
And every bride's ambition satisfied.
Where fashion or mere fantasy decrees
We shift about—all that great glory spent—
Like some poor Arab tribesman and his tent.

We were the last romantics—chose for theme
Traditional sanctity and loveliness;
Whatever's written in what poets name
The book of the people; whatever most can bless
The mind of man or elevate a rhyme.

The last lines are written by a man who sees disintegration all around him, and who has had a foretaste of death:

But all is changed, that high horse riderless,
Though mounted in that saddle Homer rode
Where the swan drifts upon a darkening flood.

The second method of expression seen in its maturity in these two books is quite the opposite of the grand historical style reflected in the lines above. It is the style of the short aphorism or wise saying. An example would be the beautiful "Gratitude to the Unknown Instructors":

What they undertook to do
They brought to pass;
All things hang like a drop of dew
Upon a blade of grass.

The final method to find its fruition in this period is
the technique of creating *personae,* figures who seem
to be dynamic spokesmen of the many voices of the poet.
We have seen early examples of this technique in those
turn-of-the-century figures: Aedh, Hanrahan, Robartes.
Now the tendency finds expression in great dialogue
poems like "The Dialogue of Self and Soul" and "Vacillation," where the two speakers seem to be contending
halves of the same personality. It also finds expression
in the creation of *persona* like Crazy Jane.

In Crazy Jane many extremes meet. She is not an ideal
figure like the figures that inhabit the moon's fifteenth
phase. She is rather an all-too-human poet's suggestion
that in the grossness of the human flesh spiritual salvation
may be found:

I met the Bishop on the road
And much said he and I.
"Those breasts are flat and fallen now,
Those veins must soon be dry;
Live in a heavenly mansion,
Not in some foul sty."

"Fair and foul are near of kin,
And fair needs foul," I cried.

"My friends are gone, but that's a truth
Nor grave nor bed denied,
Learned in bodily lowliness
And in the heart's pride.

"A woman can be proud and stiff
When on love intent;
But Love has pitched his mansion in
The place of excrement;
For nothing can be sole or whole
That has not been rent."

—"Crazy Jane Talks with the
Bishop"

One of the best-known and most intriguing of Yeats's poems of the period is "Byzantium" (1930). It is a very obscure poem, and yet it seems full of luminous meaning. Rather than join in the critical debate over its correct interpretation, let us simply attend to its last lines, where Yeats writes of the dance again, darkly symbolizing the austerity of the rhythmic creative act, which "breaks the flood" and turbulence of experience by imposing form upon that chaos:

Marbles of the dancing floor
Break bitter furies of complexity,
Those images that yet
Fresh images beget,
That dolphin-torn, that gong-tormented sea.

CHAPTER 6

The Last Years

I

N THE autumn of 1927 Yeats and his wife went from Algeciras to Seville to Cannes in France and then to Rapallo, Italy, in search of a climate that would help the poet regain his health. He continued, against doctor's orders, his study of nineteenth-century German philosophy, a study that left its mark upon the revised edition of *A Vision*.

Algeciras is on the southern coast of Spain, not far from Gibraltar. Across the Strait of Gibraltar lies the coast of North Africa. In a flight of imaginative whimsy Yeats wrote a poem that seems to suggest that the coast of Africa is the land of the dead, and himself in Algeciras

an old man waiting for death on the shores of the land
of the living:

> The heron-billed pale cattle-birds
> That feed on some foul parasite
> Of the Moroccan flocks and herds
> Cross the narrow Straits to light
> In the rich midnight of the garden trees
> Till the dawn break upon those mingled seas.

.   .   .

> Greater glory in the sun,
> An evening chill upon the air,
> Bid imagination run
> Much on the Great Questioner;
> What He can question, what if questioned I
> Can with a fitting confidence reply.

—"At Algeciras—
A Meditation Upon Death"

In a sense all Yeats's poetry after *A Vision* is a preparation for death. In these last years the preparation becomes most insistent.

Rapallo in the winter of 1928 was very pleasant for
Yeats. Ezra Pound's company made it all the more en-
joyable. Yeats decided to retire from the Senate, making
his parting speech in a visit to Ireland in March. The
Yeats children were at school in Switzerland. At the

end of the year he was back in Rapallo. He spent the summer of 1929 at Ballylee. That was his last summer there. Although the tower had served as one of his most powerful symbols, the actual building had to be abandoned because the damp did not agree with Yeats's failing health.

From here on his life becomes a depressing alternation between illness and comparative health. At Rapallo in the winter of 1929–30 he suffered from Malta fever, read detective stories, composed many of the strange aphoristic poems of *The Winding Stair*, and convalesced. At the end of June he visited Coole and his beloved Sligo. All through his travels he wrote at a great pace in a style that was now superbly controlled in its mastery over extremes of grandeur and brutality. Yeats's thoughts were with the bitter and powerful eighteenth-century Irish Protestant satirist, Jonathan Swift, the author of *Gulliver's Travels*, as he himself wrote the play *The Words upon the Window-Pane*.

It is perhaps the only Yeats play written in a prose close to realism. The central incident of the play is a slight one—some enthusiasts meet in a Dublin house for a séance, which is disturbed by an old man's unruly ghost. Yeats's knowledge of what went on at such a gathering was, of course, impeccable, and it shows in the casual detailing of the near realistic style. The bitter ghost is the spirit of Jonathan Swift. He had once lived in the house. While all the other members of the séance are anxious to drive the ghost away, two of them recognize the voice. One is young John Corbet—who is writing a dissertation on Swift at the University of Cambridge—and the other is Dr. Trench, a civilized man "of between sixty and seventy."

As usual the dramatic incident reflects a historical principle. In the Notes to the play Yeats explains the mischiefs of partisan democracy, where a man, instead of being his individual free self, becomes a blind adherent to a party:

> The Many do their day's work well, and so far from copying even the wisest of their neighbours affect 'a singularity' in action and in thought; but set them to the work of the State and every man Jack is 'listed in a party,' becomes the fanatical follower of men of whose characters he knows next to nothing, and from that day on puts nothing into his mouth that some other man has not already chewed and digested. And furthermore, from the moment of enlistment thinks himself above other men and struggles for power until all is confusion.

This is Yeats's own summary of Swift's argument in *The Discourse of the Contests and Dissensions between the Nobles and the Commons in Athens and Rome.* Yeats found in Swift and the Irish eighteenth century the last glorious development of an individualistic culture before modern man's loss of self. As he puts it, again in the Notes: "I read Swift for months together, Burke and Berkeley less often but always with excitement, and Goldsmith lures and waits. . . . I seek an image of the modern mind's discovery of itself, . . . in that one Irish century [the eighteenth] that escaped from darkness and confusion."

This, then, is the historical argument dramatized in the play: the onset of mass standardization after the individualism of the eighteenth century. The symbol is Jonathan Swift. How does Yeats work this into the dramatic incident?

Swift had two curious and overlapping love affairs with women he called Vanessa and Stella. Why did he marry neither? Why was there a question as to whether the affairs had been sexually consummated? Historians have debated over this, and it is the subject of the dissertation by Yeats's dramatis persona, John Corbet. Some suggest that Swift's incipient and finally actual syphillitic madness kept him from begetting children. Yeats presents another argument—intertwining the historical and personal—through the voice of Swift's ghost: "Am I to add another to the healthy rascaldom and knavery of the world? . . . O God, hear the prayer of Jonathan Swift, that afflicted man, and grant that he may leave posterity nothing but his intellect that came to him from Heaven." Swift's personal tragedy is transformed by Yeats into the cry of the solitary intellect rejecting the thriving soullessness ("healthy rascaldom")of democracy gone wrong.

The Swift seen by the medium in her trance is a mad and horrible old man: "His clothes were dirty, his face covered with boils. Some disease had made one of his eyes swell up, it stood out from his face like a hen's egg." "He looked like that in his old age," John Corbet murmurs. And the significance of *Words upon the Window Pane* is precisely in the shaping of the figure of a wise wild old man, a figure we shall encounter repeatedly as we move into the period of Yeats's final poetry.

The winter of 1930–31 he spent in Ireland, without any mishap, to stay by the side of the eighty-year-old Lady Gregory. He received an honorary degree from Oxford in 1931. The winter of 1931–32, the winter before Lady Gregory's death, he spent almost entirely at Coole. In the final days of her life, Yeats wrote the beautiful "Coole Park" and "Coole Park and Ballylee, 1931."

In 1932 Yeats went to America for the last time. His previous visit had been made to raise money for Thoor Ballylee. Now he hoped to raise money for the Irish Academy of Letters, which he and George Bernard Shaw had recently founded, and for the renovation of an old country house, Riversdale by name, situated a little way out of Dublin, that the Yeatses had recently acquired. Yeats traveled and was received in high style. When he toured America in 1911, he had been a writer of great promise; the next time he came, he was a writer of stature. His final tour was made as a writer who had gained international fame.

In the country comfort of Riversdale, Yeats's mind turned to imaginative political theories. His disappointment with the middle class, his experience of idealistic endeavor shattered because of adverse public opinion, mixed with the irascibility of old age, gave rise to peculiar opinions. As the noted critic Richard Ellmann has observed, Yeats's father had been right to spot in his son a streak of basic conservatism even in his most revolutionary days: "A revolutionary who puts spiritual ennoblement above political or economic gains is apt to find himself . . . on the side of the Tories [conservatives]," writes Ellmann. And so it was that Yeats now wrote enthusiastically on eugenics, the science of improving the quality of the human race by carefully selecting the parents. He also found things worthy of admiration in Fascist doctrine, and "involved himself slightly" with the Irish Blueshirts, a conservative counter-revolutionary group pledged to give service for the establishment of law-and-order in Ireland. All this doctrinaire and impractical extremism, touched by the alchemy of his imagination, produced most powerful verse, sometimes in support of violence:

> Grandfather sang it under the gallows:
> "Hear, gentlemen, ladies, and all mankind:
> Money is good and a girl might be better,
> But good strong blows are delights to the mind."
>
> —"Three Songs to the Same Tune"

Among the friends of Yeats's last years, Dorothy Wellesley occupies the place of honor. She was a young noblewoman who is now considered no more than a minor literary figure but was then a poet of some repute. While Yeats was in England, he stayed often at her estate, Penns-in-the-Rocks. They wrote poems together and exchanged many letters. Their correspondence dealt so deeply with questions about the nature of poetry that it was later to be published as *Letters on Poetry from W. B. Yeats to Dorothy Wellesley*. In fact Yeats articulated and arranged some of his aesthetic predilections through his relationship with Dorothy Wellesley. (In somewhat the same way, he had articulated and arranged his philosophical predilections in letters exchanged with his friend Thomas Sturge Moore. That correspondence, too, has been published.)

Another friend worthy of mention is the Indian monk Shri Purohit Swami. This portly, shrewd, yet simple and childlike man had come to Yeats with an account of his own teacher's miraculous pilgrimage, to that remote lake on Mount Meru that Yeats celebrates in "Supernatural Songs." The swami translated this account from Marathi into an English that profited from Yeats's revisions. *An Indian Monk* and *The Holy Mountain*, results of these labors, were published, with introductions by Yeats, in 1932 and 1934. Yeats received from Shri Purohit a kind of orthodox mystic interpretation of the Upanishads, ancient Indian philosophical texts. The nobility of the interpretation engaged his mind. With Shri Purohit he embarked upon a translation into English of the ten principal Upanishads. The resulting volume, *The Ten Principal Upanishads*, forms, with the *Aphorisms of Yoga* by Patanjali (an ancient semilegendary Indian philosopher) and Sophocles' *Oedipus Rex*, Yeats's distinguished efforts at translation. Although he was deeply interested in Indian philosophy, the glorification of ancient China and Japan is also very strong in his last poems and plays.

"Meru" is the most celebrated "Indian" poem of Yeats's last period. As the symbol of the stasis of wisdom beyond the raging cycles of history, Yeats chose the immobile sages on the peak of Meru, India's legendary holy mountain, or on Everest, the actual peak of the roof of the world:

> Civilisation is hooped together, brought
> Under a rule, under the semblance of peace
> By manifold illusion; but man's life is thought,
> And he, despite his terror, cannot cease
> Ravening through century after century,
> Ravening, raging, and uprooting that he may come
> Into the desolation of reality:
> Egypt and Greece, good-bye, and good-bye, Rome!
> Hermits upon Mount Meru or Everest,
> Caverned in night under the drifted snow,
> Or where that snow and winter's dreadful blast
> Beat down upon their naked bodies, know
> That day brings round the night, that before dawn
> His glory and his monuments are gone.

It is the final poem of his renowned "Supernatural Songs," a series of poems by a fictive speaker, Ribh, which Yeats included in his collection *A Full Moon in March* and published in 1935, just before he went with Shri Purohit to the island of Majorca off the coast of Spain. Yeats claimed that all the poems in the series reflect his affinity for India. With Ribh in mind, he wrote, "for the moment I associated early Christian Ireland with India; Shri Purohit Swami, protected during his pilgrimage to a remote Himalayan shrine by a strange great dog that disappeared when danger was past, might have been that blessed Cellach [an early Irish saint] who sang upon his deathbed of bird and beast." Yet about this particular sequence of poems Yeats also writes, "the hermit Ribh in 'Supernatural Songs' is an imaginary critic of St. Patrick. His Christianity, come perhaps from Egypt, like much early Irish Christianity, echoes pre-Christian thought." (In addition to ancient China and Japan, early Christian Byzantium, Babylon, ancient Egypt, and ancient Arabia were important locations within the symbolic and mythologic history and geography that he had written of in *A Vision* and in much of his poetry and plays.)

"An imaginary critic of St. Patrick"—Yeats had been playing with that figure ever since the 1880's. As we have seen, Oisin's loyalty to the memory of a heroic Ireland was a criticism of St. Patrick. Ribh too gets his power from heroic, pre-Christian Ireland. He speaks the opening poem of "Supernatural Songs" at the tomb of Baile and Ailinn, legendary Irish lovers. His wisdom comes, not from some ascetic spiritual source, but from the light shed by the embrace of the two ghosts on the anniversary of their death. If Crazy Jane's blunt language is a cry for salvation through the body, Ribh's saintly language is another version of that cry:

Here on the anniversary of their death,
The anniversary of their first embrace,
Those lovers, purified by tragedy,
Hurry into each other's arms; these eyes,
By water, herb, and solitary prayer
Made aquiline, are open to that light.
Though somewhat broken by the leaves, that light
Lies in a circle on the grass; therein
I turn the pages of my holy book.

—"Ribh at the Tomb of
Baile and Ailinn"

Once this personality is established, Yeats lets Ribh speak of a peculiar supernatural quality that belongs to the flesh rather than to the spirit alone. Sometimes Ribh speaks in paradoxes: "Hatred of God may bring the soul to God" ("Ribh Considers Christian Love Insufficient"). Once Ribh takes on Saint Patrick directly, criticizing the masculine Christian Trinity of Father, Son, and Holy Ghost:

An abstract Greek absurdity has crazed the man—
Recall that masculine Trinity. Man, woman, child
(a daughter or a son),
That's how all natural or supernatural stories run.

Natural and supernatural
with the self-same ring are wed. . . .

—"Ribh Denounces Patrick"

A remarkable combination of godliness and sexuality!

But perhaps the most memorable voice of wise Ribh is the aphoristic one of "There," "He and She," "Conjunctions," "A Needle's Eye." Here is "There," a picture of the Ribhean Paradise:

> There all the barrel-hoops are knit,
> There all the serpent-tails are bit,
> There all the gyres converge in one,
> There all the planets drop in the Sun.

While with the swami in Spain, Yeats fell ill with dropsy, an accumulation of excess fluid of the body. This was his last illness. For a while he recovered, and from October 1936 to December 1937 he visited Britain.

In public life Yeats was a man of importance. In 1935, the P.E.N. (Poets, Playwrights, Editors, Essayists, and Novelists) Club had given a dinner to celebrate his seventieth birthday, which many famous writers attended. Next morning the prestigious *Irish Times* published a lead article and a supplement honoring him. Yeats's earlier associate, Douglas Hyde, was now president of the Irish Republic.

Yet Yeats's relationship to his own public image was no longer as integral as it had been in youth and middle age. Perhaps the only public acts that he performed with full involvement were the editing of *The Oxford Book of Modern Verse* and the making of some radio programs for the British Broadcasting Corporation (B.B.C.).

The Oxford Book of Modern Verse (1892–1935) is an eccentric collection. Yeats worked hard on it, but he did not possess the uncommitted objective mind of the good editor. The volume came to reflect Yeats's own taste much more than it represented the range of modern English poetry. Although he claimed to be impartial, his choice of modern poetry was selected very much on the basis of his own taste. Yeats had set himself a personal problem: " 'How far do I like the Ezra [Pound], Auden, Eliot school, and if I do not, why not?' Then he posed this further problem: 'Why do the younger generation like it so much? What do they see or hope?' " The introduction to *The Oxford Book* provides Yeats's answers to these problems.

He gave his first radio broadcast on B.B.C. on October 20, 1936. He had just turned seventy-one. His subject was modern poetry. He found the situation of the solitary speaker confronting an invisible audience so satisfactory that he arranged for two further twenty-minute programs: "The Poet's Pub," and "The Poet's Garden." His sense that poetry had a rougher as well as a more refined voice is shown in the distinction he made between the kinds of poetry to be included in the two programs. "The Poet's Pub" was to contain popular poems, ballads, vigorous songs employing the common voice and the themes of the body. "The Poet's Garden" was to contain "purer" lyrics of a less embodied music. He chose poems by many modern writers for the two broadcasts. He rehearsed very carefully with a group of readers, trying to put into practice his theories about reading poetry aloud that had now become firm convictions. Unfortunately the records of the broadcasts did not survive the Second World War.

Yeats wrote some very fine plays during these final years. *The Resurrection, Purgatory, The Death of Cuchulain*—to choose the best—each seem to have a distinctive and startling excellence of its own.

On Easter Sunday, two young disciples of Christ—a Greek and a Jew—are discussing Jesus. This is the opening scene of *The Resurrection*. The Greek thinks of Him as a god who played the part of a man, and the Jew as "the best man who ever lived," but one who, because of his consuming pity for human suffering, had mistaken himself for the Messiah. As usual Yeats is trying to distill the essences of two great civilizations in a conversation between two individuals. The rationality of the Greek, who sees the supernatural and the natural as distinct and never organically unified, is contrasted to the Jew's resistance to the imaging of God. In an adjoining room eleven apostles are sitting in poses of extreme dejection. Out in the streets, the frenzied festival procession of the semi-Asian Greek god Dionysos is talking place. The festival celebrates the resurrection of the dead Dionysos, god of wine, song, and sexual energy. Perhaps Yeats is trying to suggest that, just as the regeneration of Dionysos belonged to a sex-centered cycle of history, the regeneration of Christ heralds the opposite, spirit-centered cycle.

A Syrian disciple runs in with the news that Christ

has risen. The Jew and the Greek question him until the risen Christ appears in the room. Christ's costume is in keeping with the Noh tradition; he wears "a recognisable but stylistic mask." The Greek, confident that the figure is totally supernatural, goes up to it to test that confidence. Yeats gives us the mystery of Christ's human-divine being in a superbly conceived exclamation of fascinated horror uttered by the Greek: "The heart of a phantom is beating! . . . O Athens, Alexandria, Rome, something has come to destroy you."

Purgatory dramatizes the theme of the middle section of *A Vision*—"the soul in judgment." The tone of the play is eerie. An old man and a boy—father and son—watch a ruined house. Slowly the house comes to life, lights appear in the window and the old man's dead parents re-enact the night of the old man's begetting. The husband had come home drunk that night and his highborn wife had desired him. The old man watches that long-past coupling with loathing, for his mother had died at his birth and his drunken father had kept him uneducated. When he was sixteen the old man had murdered his father and then set fire to the house to conceal his crime. He now tells his own son—the boy—this story, and observes that "the souls in Purgatory . . . come back to habitations and familiar spots." That is indeed the reason for this re-enactment. The soul of the mother, filled with remorse at having borne her husband's murderer to satisfy her own sexual longing, must keep a ghostly anniversary of that night every year. The half-mad old man fancies that if he can end his father's line there will be no need for his mother to suffer in purgatory any more. He kills his son with the same knife that he had used on his father. The language of the play becomes limpid with adoration as the old man imagines his mother's soul saved, freed from the years of remorse:

> . . . study that tree.
> It stands there like a purified soul,
> All cold, sweet, glistening light.
> Dear mother, the window is dark again,
> But you are in the light because
> I finished all that consequence.
> I killed that lad because had he grown up
> He would have struck a woman's fancy,
> Begot, and passed pollution on.
> I am a wretched foul old man
> And therefore harmless.

But his logic is faulty, of course. He hears once again the hoofbeats of his murdered father's horse. The play closes with his cry of anguish:

> Twice a murderer and all for nothing,
> And she must animate that dead night
> Not once but many times!
> O God,
> Release my mother's soul from that dream!
> Mankind can do no more. Appease
> The misery of the living
> and the remorse of the dead.

Early in life Yeats had determined to write plays that would go beyond realism. The Noh with its ghostly actors had helped him develop such a form, as had his own interest in the occult. In every play he tried to touch some level of consciousness deeper than our everyday one. In *Purgatory* one feels the presence of what Sigmund Freud has called the Oedipal drive—a son's sexual love for his mother, his envy of his potent father, of his own potent son, and his desire to keep his mother unviolated.

The Death of Cuchulain is Yeats's last play. He made changes in it on his deathbed. There seems something grimly appropriate in the heroic old poet dying as he rehearses in the imagination the death of his hero. As in *On Baile's Strand*, that play about Cuchulain written so many years ago, Yeats places the solemn and tragic action within a frame of folk drama.

Within the central action, Cuchulain goes offstage to fight a battle that he knows means certain death for him. He receives six mortal wounds and staggers back onstage to tie himself to a pillar, so that he can die a hero's death, standing. Queen Aoife (pronounced *Eé-feh*), his old enemy and lover, mother of the son Cuchulain killed in *On Baile's Strand*, is there beside him. She wants to give him his death wound. But a blind beggar comes onstage and Aoife hides. The beggar kills Cuchulain in exchange for a reward of twelve pennies. Is Yeats trying to suggest that death, even a hero's death, robs man of all dignity and glory? We are reminded of the phrase he had used in 1917 at the death of young Robert Gregory: "The discourtesy of death."

The framing action that opens the play is the speech of an Old Man, the supposed producer of the play. It is a long and interesting speech, presenting Yeats's ideas about play production in a racy, outrageous idiom. A few lines from it will give its flavor:

> When they told me that I could have my own way, I wrote certain guidelines on a bit of newspaper. I wanted an audience of fifty or a hundred, and if there are more, I beg them not to shuffle their feet or talk when the actors are speaking. . . . They must know the old epics and Mr. Yeats's plays about them.

By opening the play with a contemporary old man who admires the past, Yeats is also framing the ancient world within modern realities. He is in fact dramatizing the proper interpretation and reception of the past by the modern imagination. The end of the play is in keeping with this. Queen Emer, Cuchulain's widow, is dancing on the stage with a stylized representation of his severed head. The stage darkens, she disappears, and, as the stage lights come on, the music changes to the loud "music of some Irish Fair of our day." A street singer begins to sing. In the song, writing in a sexually charged style, Yeats compares the reception of the past by the present to an act of sex. The difficulty of that reception is given thus:

> The harlot sang to the beggar-man
> I meet them face to face,
> Conall, Cuchulain, Usna's boys,
> All that most ancient race
>
> .   .   .
>
> I adore those clever eyes,
> Those muscular bodies, but can get
> No grip upon their thighs.

It is the creative poetic imagination that is most success-ful in vivifying the past. In four bold lines describing Cuchulain's body, Yeats sings a deserved and oblique song of praise to his own genius:

> No body like his body
> Had modern woman borne,
> But an old man looking on life
> Imagines it in scorn.

The mood of the last years of Yeats's poetry is not what one expects from a comfortably aging man. He had spent his youth dreaming, his middle age held captive by his devotion to Maud Gonne. At fifty-two he had married a woman half his age. Emotionally he had heard a father's guiding voice until he was nearly sixty. All this made the coming of old age seem a monstrous in-justice: he had never really experienced his prime. In his seventieth year he voluntarily underwent surgery to restore his sexual energy. When friends complained about the tones of "lust and rage" that pervaded his poetry, he wrote the famous quatrain:

You think it horrible that lust and rage
Should dance attention upon my old age;
They were not such a plague when I was young;
What else have I to spur me into song?

     —"The Spur"

These poems of lust and rage fall into two groups:
his last collection—*New Poems*—which he saw through
the press in January 1938; and the final uncollected
poems. The two groups have now been put together
as *Last Poems*.

   Grant me an old man's frenzy,
   Myself must I remake. . . .

     —"An Acre of Grass"

That is the chief theme of *New Poems:* an assessment
of the past, the forging of a new personality to meet
death. The language is often stripped to a surprising
bareness, the kind of poetry that is most difficult to
write. The poems are not only good words arranged
harmoniously to entertain and profit others, but the cry
of the poet's own spirit, concerned with its own final
meaning.

   All his happier dreams came true—
   A small old house, wife, daughter, son,
   Grounds where plum and cabbage grew,
   Poets and Wits about him drew;
   "What then?" sang Plato's ghost. "What then?"

     —"What Then?"

He questions the ancestors whom he had sought to pla-
cate twenty years ago in *Responsibilities*.

> I call on those that call me son,
> Grandson, or great-grandson,
> On uncles, aunts, great-uncles or great-aunts,
> To judge what I have done.
> Have I, that put it into words,
> Spoilt what old loins have sent?
> Eyes spiritualised by death can judge,
> I cannot, but I am not content.
>
> —"Are You Content?"

In "Beautiful Lofty Things," the grandeur of memory
combines consolation and a sense of loss:

> Beautiful lofty things: O'Leary's noble head;
> My father upon the Abbey stage,
>   before him a raging crowd:
> "This Land of Saints,"
>   and then as the applause died out,
> "Of plaster saints"; his beautiful
>   mischievous head thrown back.
> Standish O'Grady supporting himself
>   between the tables
> Speaking to a drunken audience
>   high nonsensical words;
> Augusta Gregory seated at her
>   great ormolu table,
> Her eightieth winter approaching:
>   "Yesterday he threatened my life.

I told him that nightly from six to seven
    I sat at this table,
The blinds drawn up"; Maud Gonne
    at Howth station waiting a train,
Pallas Athene in that straight back
    and arrogant head:
All the Olympians; a thing never known again.

Sometimes the solution to the bitterness of old age seems to lie in identifying his own predicament with the predicament of the world. As we have seen in *A Vision*, and the poems of the Civil War, this is a typically Yeatsian gesture.

With Dorothy Wellesley he wrote a ballad sequence, "The Three Bushes." The crystalline yet open sexuality of these poems is again typical of the final Yeats.

Bird sighs for the air,
Thought for I know not where,
For the womb the seed sighs.
Now sinks the same rest
On mind, on nest,
On straining thighs.

    —"The Lover's Song"

A strange, young, half-crazed actress—Margot Ruddock—came into his life for a few months at this time. Yeats's gentleness toward her shows itself in the little poem "Sweet Dancer":

If strange men come from the house
To lead her away, do not say
That she is happy being crazy;
Lead them gently astray;
Let her finish her dance,
Let her finish her dance.
Ah, dancer, ah, sweet dancer!

It is a matter of awed surprise that the poems that Yeats wrote after this last book should contain some of his best work. Once again the two poles emerge. At one end is the amazing self-confident simplicity of, say, "The Statesman's Holiday," where Yeats celebrates the wise joy of renouncing an active career and wooing irresponsibility in old age:

With boys and girls about him
With any sort of clothes,
With a hat out of fashion,
With old patched shoes,
With ragged bandit cloak,
With an eye like a hawk,
With a stiff straight back,
With a strutting turkey walk,
With a bag full of pennies,
With a monkey on a chain,
With a great cock's feather,
With an old foul tune.
Tall dames go walking in grass-green Avalon.

The same careless yet achieved simplicity is there in

"News for the Delphic Oracle," where Yeats teaches the ancient oracle of Apollo at Delphi that visions of the supernatural need not be solemn or antiseptic:

> Down the mountain walls
> From where Pan's cavern is
> Intolerable music falls.
> Foul goat-head, brutal arm appear,
> Belly, shoulder, bum,
> Flash fishlike; nymphs and satyrs
> Copulate in the foam.

The powerful simplicity is there in "High Talk," where Yeats deliberately breaks the rhythm to mock his own grand style as a species of walking on stilts:

> Malachi Stilt-Jack am I,
>   whatever I learned has run wild,
> From collar to collar, from stilt to stilt,
>   from father to child.
> All metaphor, Malachi, stilts and all. . . .

But at the other pole of the language of these final poems, the old grandeur lingers still. It flashes as Yeats recalls Padraic Pearse, martyr of the long-past Easter 1916:

> When Pearse summoned Cuchulain to his side,
> What stalked through the Post Office? What intellect,
> What calculation, number, measurement, replied?
>
>   —"The Statues"

And it shows, for example, in the calm dignity of "Long-Legged Fly":

> That civilisation may not sink,
> Its great battle lost,
> Quiet the dog, tether the pony
> To a distant post;
> Our master Caesar is in the tent
> Where the maps are spread,
> His eyes fixed upon nothing,
> A hand under his head.
> *Like a long-legged fly upon the stream*
> *His mind moves upon silence.*

In "The Circus Animals' Desertion," he relates the present state of his imagination to his past. All his life he has worked with dreams or symbols that inhabit or grow in his "pure mind"—occupy, that is to say, an area of the mind that is remote from the rough-and-tumble of actual experience. Now, with old age, his imaginative ladder to that remote upper story of the mind is gone. He either cannot or will not summon up new dreams and symbols. Now he must find his themes at the source of dreams and symbols—the raw experience of the heart:

> . . . Now that my ladder's gone,
> I must lie down where all the ladders start,
> In the foul rag-and-bone shop of the heart.

Yeats spent the summer of 1938 in England and Ireland. It was a time for farewells. Maud Gonne came to visit him in Riversdale. They talked in peace this last time and on Yeats's side, at least, with a sense of much meaningless suffering in the past. The meeting echoes through his very last poem about her, "A Bronze Head":

> But even at the starting-post, all sleek and new,
> I saw the wildness in her and I thought
> A vision of terror that it must live through
> Had shattered her soul. . . .

In August what turned out to be a valedictory festival took place at the Abbey Theatre: a performance of *Purgatory*, "revivals of *On Baile's Strand* and other early masterpieces, and lectures . . . on phases and figures of the Irish Dramatic Movement." In October he received the news of the death of his old friend Olivia Shakespear. Soon after, he left for Cap Martin on the warm and beautiful southern coast of France.

He looked well and happy in his rooms at the Hôtel Idéal Séjour. He was writing poetry. All his life he had tried to make life into myth. In the voice of the Old Man who speaks the Prologue of *The Death of Cuchulain*, one hears Yeats's own voice: "I belong to mythology." Reading the two poems that he wrote during these last days of his life, one is prepared to agree that life and myth had finally come together in Yeats. One of them, "Cuchulain Comforted," describes Cuchulain's entry into the next world. The other, "The Black Tower," is a defiant and obscure cry, uttered in darkness, that, though the king is dead, the soldiers will continue to guard the tower: "Stand we on guard oath-bound!" There is also the testimony of his last letter: "It seems to me that I have found what I wanted. When I try to put all into a phrase I say, 'Man can embody truth but he cannot know it.' I must embody it in the completion of my life."

He died on January 28, 1939. He was buried in the little nearby town of Roquebrune. The outbreak of the Second World War brought to a halt plans for bringing his body to Ireland. Then in 1948 the poet's grave was opened, and the coffin was brought to Sligo. He lies, as he wished, in Drumcliff churchyard. In his own words:

> Under bare Ben Bulben's head
> In Drumcliff churchyard Yeats is laid.
> An ancestor was rector there
> Long years ago, a church stands near,
> By the road an ancient cross.
> No marble, no conventional phrase;
> On limestone quarried near the spot
> By his command these words are cut:
> > *Cast a cold eye*
> > *On life, on death.*
> > *Horseman, pass by!*
>
> —"Under Ben Bulben"

CHAPTER 7
The Poet's
Achievement

WHAT constitutes the uniqueness of a writer? The ways in which he is new and the ways in which he relates to the old. To put it differently, a writer's uniqueness lies in his originality and in his relationship to tradition. Let us consider Yeats's achievement in its newness and in its reassertion of the old.

Any such catalogue should begin with Yeats's contributions to the Irish literary renaissance. It was his belief that Ireland was ready for a regeneration of the spirit in 1891, when, after the death of the great Irish political leader Charles Stewart Parnell, a political regeneration seemed impossible. But a country does not achieve a spiritual rebirth simply because the time is ripe. A propitious time may come to nothing without the vision to give it direction. Yeats declared that the Irish people must rediscover their own roots and heritage.

For Yeats, as we have seen, these roots of Irish identity were to be found primarily in pre-Christian myth, not only in particular mythic stories like those of Oisin and Cuchulain but in the general sense of a mythic past. That a nation might find its roots in its earliest legends may seem obvious to us, but in Yeats's time the work of researching and translating the ancient myths of Ireland was an academic pursuit, the life work of scholars. Lady Gregory was herself unique in trying to change that scene with her amateur collections of folklore, and her books of popularized mythology like *Cuchulain of Miurthemne*. But Yeats's genius added something only genius can add. He gave the myth a present reality. He transformed a corner of Irish legend—especially the story of Cuchulain—into a lasting symbol of the possibility of heroism in modern Ireland. The Irishman, who from the nineteenth century on had recognized himself in literature as a sentimental creature, simple, poetic, hotheaded, credulous, and tipsy—in fact, Yeats himself sometimes presented a representative Irishman surprisingly close to this one—could find in the mythic past a new image of himself.

The second place where Yeats found Irish roots is to many people a surprise: in the Irish eighteenth century. This was indeed a period of intellectual, artistic, and social achievement among the Anglo-Irish ascendancy. But it was not a time of especial glory for the native

Irish, who were Catholic. But it is not a poet's obligation to be historically accurate, and Yeats does make us feel that some secret of excellence in Ireland as a whole lay in that period.

This, then, is one aspect of Yeats's reassertion of the old: to forge an Irish identity out of pre-Christian myth and the Anglo-Irish eighteenth century.

As he sought out these roots he also looked into modern European literature. If the former gave depth to Irish writing, the latter gave breadth.

Europe gave Yeats Symbolism—writing that does not try to describe reality exactly but rather tries to suggest its meaning through the use of symbols. It is a writing that considers the things of the natural world to be a collection of symbols, like words in a dictionary, that can be arranged by the poet in new ways to suggest significance beyond that world. Symbolism originated in France around the middle of the nineteenth century. Certainly most fashionable British writers had been aware of it and had even played with it for well over a generation before Yeats. But once again it is Yeats who caught and used the mode most successfully in his poems and plays. A line such as "Great Powers of falling wave and wind and windy fire" ("The Poet Pleads to the Elemental Powers") seems to have that delicate indirection that the best Symbolist poetry possesses. And that indirection survives in lines such as the following, appearing among all the blunt directness of his last style: *"There in the tomb stand the dead upright, / But winds come up from the shore—"* ("The Black Tower") although he himself believed, as he wrote to Dorothy Wellesley, that he had left Symbolism behind with his early poetry: "It shows me the road I and others of my time went for certain furlongs. It is not the way I go now. . . ."

Whatever might have been the chronology of Symbolism in his verse, he certainly never left it behind in his plays. And in choosing to write Symbolist and ritual-like drama, he placed the Irish theatre within a European controversy. In the closing years of the last century and the opening of the present, serious theatre in Europe was divided into two camps. On one side was the kind of drama that made the stage appear as lifelike as possible; the themes of the plays were topical psychological and social issues. This tendency, as we saw earlier, was identified with its best practitioner, Henrik Ibsen. On the other side was Symbolist drama which, like Symbolist poetry, tried to present and evoke realities beyond the scope of the discursive intellect. Yeats knew this drama best through the work of Villiers de l'Isle Adam, Emile Verhaeren, and Maurice Maeterlinck. In seeking to combine the Symbolist technique with the rich tradition of Irish humor and folk drama, Yeats did indeed extend the limits of his country's culture.

But he did not stop with Western Europe alone. He was open to the waves of Eastern influence that were breaking on Western shores at the time. Some of it he received through his preoccupation with spiritism. But his attempts at seeing things through Indian, Chinese, and Japanese eyes pays tribute to the flexibility of his imagination. We have already looked at the poetry of his "Indian" phase, and at the importance of the Japanese Noh play in his work. Let us look at an example of his celebration of the "tragic joy" that he understood to be essential to the way of ancient China. Here he describes a piece of carved semiprecious blue stone called lapis lazuli:

> Two Chinamen, behind them a third,
> Are carved in lapis lazuli,
> Over them flies a long-legged bird,
> A symbol of longevity;
> The third, doubtless a serving-man,
> Carries a musical instrument.
>
> Every discoloration of the stone,
> Every accidental crack or dent,
> Seems a water-course or an avalanche,
> Or lofty slope where it still snows
> Though doubtless plum or cherry-branch
> Sweetens the little half-way house
> Those Chinamen climb towards, and I
> Delight to imagine them seated there;
> There, on the mountain and the sky,
> On all the tragic scene they stare.
> One asks for mournful melodies;
> Accomplished fingers begin to play.
> Their eyes mid many wrinkles, their eyes,
> Their ancient, glittering eyes, are gay.
>
> —"Lapis Lazuli"

The Indian sages on Meru had learned to go beyond all civilizations to find self-transcendence. The Chinese wise men upon this imaginary mountainside remain attached to civilization's "tragic scene." They achieve "gaiety"—Yeats's simple word for a sort of transcendence—through the harmony of art. Yeats places them within an art object: they are carved upon the stone, itself a product of a highly civilized culture. And within the world of the lapis lazuli, yet another harmony is introduced: the gaiety of the old men rises in response to an imagined music.

So much for Yeats's relationship to Irish literature and to an Irish self-concept. There is a mixture of old and new also in the work of Yeats the individual poet.

He conceived of poetry as the business of soul-making, not merely as a rhetorical exercise. And in slowly modeling his verse to reflect his changing self, he successfully practiced many different styles. Perhaps the earliest dreaming verse owed too much to the existing style of Pre-Raphaelite poetry. But Yeats was at least a major Pre-Raphaelite; and that dreaming stance, longing for an ideal beauty lodged outside this world, was a genuine one.

As Yeats moved into middle age and his dreams left him, his poetry changed correspondingly. This sounds a simple enough statement, but the achievement itself is a very difficult one. The phenomenon of an aging poet tied to a youthful style is embarrassingly frequent. That Yeats's style did change with the movement of his self shows both a real connection between self and style in his work and Yeats's command over his medium. For if the former is not true, if there is no connection between self and style, the change in a man's being makes no difference to the way he writes, and if the latter is not present, if the poet has no command over his medium, he cannot change his way with words even if he wants to.

In his later style Yeats turned to many traditional forms of poetry and made them new. The public voice of poetry, where a poet is not merely presenting his personal experience but speaking as a member of a particular society, used so much in the earlier centuries of English literature by poets such as Donne, Milton, Dryden, Pope, and Wordsworth, had become too remote and perhaps even institutionalized in poets of the nineteenth century such as Alfred Tennyson and Matthew Arnold. It had become merely public, lacking in that personal, even idiosyncratic element that, paradoxically enough, makes such poetry compelling. Fresh from his disappointments in the political arena, Yeats used the public voice with a ring of bitter, sometimes grotesque sincerity that transformed it almost completely, and gave the young poets of the 1930's a style to emulate. Here are two examples of that voice, from 1914 to 1938, showing its slow liberation from the dreaming, private one. In the first, in a style still very close to the overelaborate earlier style, Yeats expresses a contempt for public opinion that is hardly comprehensible. In the second, the voice is so direct that there is no mistaking its meaning:

While I, from that reed-throated whisperer
Who comes at need, although not now as once
A clear articulation in the air,
But inwardly, surmise companions
Beyond the fling of the dull ass's hoof
—Ben Jonson's phrase—and find when June is come
At Kyle-na-no under the ancient roof
A sterner conscience and a friendlier home,
I can forgive even that wrong of wrongs,
Those undreamt accidents that have made me
—Seeing that Fame has perished this long while,
Being but a part of ancient ceremony—
Notorious, till all my priceless things
Are but a post the passing dogs defile, . . .

        —"While I, from
           That Reed-Throated Whisperer"

Irish poets, learn your trade,
Sing whatever is well made,

     .   .   .

Sing the peasantry, and then
Hard-riding country gentlemen,
The holiness of monks, and after
Porter-drinker's randy laughter;
Sing the lords and ladies gay
That were beaten into the clay
Through seven heroic centuries;
Cast your mind on other days
That we in coming days may be
Still the indomitable Irishry.

        —"Under Ben Bulben"

In the later style, the personal voice, too, was rescued from its dreams and turned to the actualities of auto-biography. Such a personal voice is characteristic of English poetry, especially English Romantic poetry in the Wordsworthian tradition. But here again, Yeats did something radically new with it. He used curious par-ticular references to personal chronology that brought a surprising quality to his poems. Lines like "Although I have come close on forty-nine / I have no child, I have nothing but a book," "I wrote it all out twenty years ago," "*Fifteen apparitions have I seen; / The Worst a coat upon a coat-hanger,*" culminate in that posthumous dec-laration, "Under bare Ben Bulben's head / In Drumcliff churchyard Yeats is laid."

Another aspect of Yeats's style that strengthened and renovated tradition is its visionary quality. The kind of imagination that could entertain the possibility of the supernatural had become extinct in the overrationalistic Victorian age. The imaginative fancifulness of the Pre-Raphaelites was largely an imitation of real vision. For the capacity of vision is a gift that cannot usually be duplicated by conscious effort. The great visionary poems of Yeats—like "The Magi," "The Double Vision of Mi-chael Robartes," "Vacillation," "Nineteen Hundred and Nineteen," "Byzantium," "Among School Children," "The Black Tower"—belong with the visionary poems of Thomas Traherne, William Blake, and William Words-worth. Yeats catches the excitement and vulnerability of the visionary moment in these characteristically simple lines from "Vacillation":

> While on the shop and street I gazed
> My body of a sudden blazed;
> And twenty minutes more or less
> It seemed, so great my happiness,
> That I was blessèd and could bless.

But this simple language is not the only one Yeats used to express visions. His interest in the occult byways of human wisdom led to the development of a genuinely allegorical language; a language, that is, where each thing stands for something else, is a sign for something else— the moon for the self looking into itself, for example, and the sun for all that is outside of the self: God, Nature, Law. The language of allegory had become unfashionable. People thought of it as a mechanical one-to-one kind of relationship. But good allegorical reading is as concentratedly creative an act as a musician's interpretation of a musical score, whereas bad allegorical reading sees only a lifeless correspondence. Yeats understood this. He wrote with the confidence of the traditional poet: those who love my work will know me whole. It was an act of revolt against the contemporary fragmented approach to literature "That book is intended . . . for my 'schoolmates only,' " he wrote of *A Vision* in 1937, at the conclusion of a general introduction to all his work. The sentence applies to his allegorical poetry as well. One must indeed endeavor to travel the paths Yeats's strange mind traveled before one can enjoy the full flavor of magnificent and cryptic lines like the following:

In pity for man's darkening thought
He walked the room and issued thence
In Galilean turbulence;
The Babylonian starlight brought
A fabulous, formless darkness in;
Odour of blood when Christ was slain
Made all Platonic tolerance vain
And vain all Doric discipline.

—"Two Songs from a Play"

Another unique Yeats product is the aphorism—the short, wise saying exemplified by the proverb. Once again the sources of this way of writing are hidden in tradition. And once again Yeats made it outrageously new. We have commented on the aphorisms in *Supernatural Songs*. But Yeats's aphorisms are spread throughout his work. When Yeats writes: "Man is in love and loves what vanishes, / What more is there to say?" ("Nineteen Hundred and Nineteen"), one feels the thrust of the real aphorism: a conviction that the statement is true, and that its seeming transparency conceals great depths of meaning.

Some critics are convinced that Yeats is the only successful modern balladeer. Most modern exercises in the ballad form seem phony and coy, and perhaps there is some coyness in Yeats's very early ballads, where the poet tried to be deliberately Irish. But he developed the ballad into a special language of self-expression. Listening to

> *"I am of Ireland,*
> *And the Holy Land of Ireland,*
> *And time runs on," cried she.*
> *"Come out of charity,*
> *Come dance with me in Ireland"*
>
> —" 'I am of Ireland' "

in the incomparable voice of the Irish actress Siobhan MacKenna, one realizes with what mastery Yeats used that form in which poets of an earlier time composed songs for the voice of a minstrel.

All these achievements in original and traditional forms were sustained by a solid virtue—awareness of the minutest particulars of his medium. He would throw the rhythmic emphasis upon what we usually consider the least beautiful parts of language so that the reader feels the function of the most skeletal of words—conjunctions, prepositions, and so forth. Lines such as the following illustrate this peculiarly Yeatsian virtue; the utilitarian words that receive rhythmic stress have been italicized: "*Until* imagination brought / A fitter welcome . . ." ("In Memory of Major Robert Gregory"); "And *therefore* I have sailed the seas and come / To the holy city of Byzantium" ("Sailing to Byzantium"); *Thereupon,* / Propped upon my two knees, / I kissed a stone ("Crazy Jane on the Mountain"). One could pile instance upon instance. They are woven into the very fabric of Yeats's verse.

Here he stands then, this giant at the head of our

century. His echo can be heard in nearly any literary artist of our time who respects tradition. Perhaps most specifically in the allegoric world view of Jorge Luis Borges, the comic fools of Samuel Beckett, the early poetry of W. H. Auden, and in the work of Theodore Roethke, Stephen Spender, and, closer to our time, W. S. Merwin, Galway Kinnell, and Michael Dennis Browne. The influence of Yeats is implicit, is found in rhythm, image, turn of phrase; but sometimes a poet openly acknowledges his debt, as Theodore Roethke does in these famous lines:

> I take this cadence from a man named Yeats;
> I take it, and I give it back again:
> For other tunes and other wanton beats
> Have tossed my heart
>   and fiddled through my brain.
> Yes, I was dancing-mad, and how
> That came to be the bears and Yeats would know.
>
> —"Four for Sir John Davies:
> I. The Dance"

But Yeats's measure is not only in his great achievements, nor in his great influence. To take that measure we have to go back to the statement with which we began this discussion of Yeats's individual style. His greatness lies in how serious a business poetry was for him, how totally life and poetry were conjoined in him. Some say he was a pompous, credulous, vain man. But that pomposity, credulousness, and vanity became transmuted in his work into eloquence. Perhaps Yeats's true precursor is another excellent yet vain poet, whom we have already cited, and whom Yeats never really liked—William Wordsworth. Wordsworth studied his own interior life, and he wrote a majestic poem, "The Prelude," subtitled "Growth of a Poet's Mind." In his verse, prose, and drama, Yeats has also left us a deliberate chronicle of the growth of a poet's mind. In his own words:

> *The friends that have it I do wrong*
> *When ever I remake a song,*
> *Should know what issue is at stake:*
> *It is myself that I remake.*

A Selected
Bibliography

BY YEATS

The Autobiography of William Butler Yeats. New York, Macmillan Company, 1953.

Collected Plays of W. B. Yeats. New York, Macmillan Company, 1953.

Collected Poems of W. B. Yeats. New York, Macmillan Company, 1956.

The Letters of W. B. Yeats, ed. Allan Wade. London, Rupert Hart-Davis, 1954.

Essays and Introductions. New York, Collier Books, 1968.

Explorations. New York, Macmillan Company, 1963.

Mythologies. New York, Collier Books, 1969.

A Vision. New York, Macmillan Company, 1969.

ABOUT YEATS

BIOGRAPHIES

Ellmann, Richard. *Yeats: The Man and the Masks.* New York, Macmillan Company, 1948.
Hone, Joseph M. *W. B. Yeats: 1865-1939.* New York, St. Martin's Press, 1962.

SOME CRITICAL WORKS OF INTEREST

Bloom, Harold. *Yeats.* New York, Oxford University Press, 1970.
De Man, Paul. "Symbolic Landscape in Wordsworth and Yeats" in Brower, Reuben A., and Poirier, Richard, eds., *In Defense of Reading: A Reader's Approach to Literary Criticism.* New York, E. P. Dutton & Co., 1962.
Donoghue, Denis, and Mulryne, J. R., eds. *An Honoured Guest: New Essays on W. B. Yeats.* London, Edward Arnold, 1965.
Ellmann, Richard. *The Identity of Yeats.* New York, Oxford University Press, 1954.
Engelberg, Edward. *The Vast Design: Patterns in W. B. Yeats's Aesthetic.* Toronto, University of Toronto Press, 1964.
Frye, Northrop. "Yeats and the Language of Symbolism" in *Fables of Identity: Studies in Poetic Mythology.* New York, Harcourt, Brace, Jovanovich, 1963.
Grossman, Allen R. *Poetic Knowledge in the Early Yeats: A Study of The Wind Among the Reeds.* Charlottesville, University Press of Virginia, 1969.
Hall, James, and Steinmann, Martin, eds. *The Permanence of Yeats: Selected Criticism.* New York, Peter Smith, 1950.
Henn, Thomas Rice. *The Lonely Tower: Studies in the Poetry of W. B. Yeats.* New York, Barnes & Noble, 1965.

Keane, Patrick J., ed. *William Butler Yeats.* New York, Mc-Graw-Hill Book Company, 1973.

Marcus, Phillip L. *Yeats and the Beginning of the Irish Renaissance.* Ithaca, Cornell University Press, 1970.

Parkinson, Thomas. W. B. Yeats: *Self-Critic: A Study of His Early Verse and the Later Poetry.* Berkeley, University of California Press, 1971.

Unterecker, John. *A Reader's Guide to William Butler Yeats.* New York, Farrar, Straus and Giroux, 1959.

————, ed. *Yeats: A Collection of Critical Essays.* Englewood, New Jersey, Prentice-Hall, 1963.

Whitaker, Thomas R. *Swan and Shadow: Yeats's Dialogue with History.* Chapel Hill, University of North Carolina Press, 1964.

Index

About the Author

Gayatri Chakravorty Spivak received her B.A. from the University of Calcutta, India, and her M.A. and Ph.D. from Cornell University. While she was a research student at Girton College, University of Cambridge, in England, she studied Yeats's poetry under the supervision of the eminent Anglo-Irish scholar, T. R. Henn. She is the author of a number of critical essays on Yeats and other modern writers, and is currently Associate Professor of English and Comparative Literature at the University of Iowa. She and her husband, the writer Talbot Spivak, live in Iowa City, Iowa.

Library of Congress Cataloging in Publication Data

Spivak, Gayatri Chakravorty.
  Myself must I remake.

    SUMMARY: A biography of the Irish
poet, dramatist, and essayist generally considered the most important poet in English
of his time.
    Bibliography: p.
    1. Yeats, William Butler, 1865–1939–
Juvenile lit. [1. Yeats, William Butler,
1865–1939. 2. Poets, Irish] I. Title.
PR5906.S6 1974   821'.8 [B] [92]   73–16343
ISBN 0–690–00114–2